Oxfordshire
and Berkshire

ORDNANCE SURVEY HISTORICAL GUIDES

Oxfordshire and Berkshire

James Bond
and Luke Over

GEORGE PHILIP

ORDNANCE SURVEY

First published in Great Britain in 1988 by George Philip & Son Ltd,
27A Floral Street,
London   WC2E 9DP
and Ordnance Survey,
Romsey Road,
Southampton SO9 4DH

Copyright © The maps in this publication are reproduced from Ordnance Survey maps with the permission of the Controller of HMSO. Crown copyright reserved. 1988

Text © James Bond and Luke Over   1988

British Library Cataloguing in Publication Data

Bond, James, *1944–*
    Oxfordshire and Berkshire.—(Ordnance survey historic county guides).
    1. Berkshire—Historical geography
    2. Oxfordshire—Historical geography
    I. Title.   II. Over, Luke   III. Series
    911′.4229   DA670.B4

    ISBN 0-540-01136-3

Filmset by Tameside Filmsetting Ltd,
Ashton-under-Lyne, Lancashire
Printed by BAS Printers Ltd,
Over Wallop, Hampshire
Bound by Robert Hartnoll Ltd
Bodmin, Cornwall

Picture acknowledgements

The illustrations in this book are reproduced by kind permission of the following:
Oxfordshire County Libraries: pp 7, 12, 39, 45, 58, 62, 72, 79 (top), 80, 116, 119 (top), 129
Department of Museum Services, Oxfordshire County Museum: p 18
Joan Brasnett: pp 46, 60, 65, 79 (bottom), 83, 84, 86, 118, 119 (bottom)
Berkshire Archaeological Association: pp 74 (top), 78 (top), 92, 97 (bottom), 101, 103, 113, 120 (top), 121, 125, 128 (top), 134, 137, 139, 145
Peter J. Foote: pp 74 (bottom), 78 (bottom), 93, 94, 95, 97 (top), 99, 105, 106, 120 (bottom), 124, 126, 128 (bottom), 131, 137, 138, 153 (top)
Berkshire County Libraries: pp 27, 143, 153 (bottom)

Endpapers: *Streatley c1875–85.*

Half title: *Bray in the late nineteenth century.*

Frontispiece: *Oxford High Street in the 1890s.*

Contents

⸻◇◇◇⸻

Oxfordshire

Stanton Harcourt at the turn of the century

THE HISTORIC COUNTY OF OXFORDSHIRE occupies just under 195ha (750 square miles) of countryside in the south midlands of England. The River Thames forms its southern border for 124km (77 miles) between Lechlade and Henley. In the north-west its boundary follows the crest of the Edgehill ridge. Elsewhere Oxfordshire is largely without natural boundaries and irregularly shaped, narrowing near Oxford itself to a central waist only 11km (7 miles) across. Apart from the nineteenth-century tidying-up of minor enclaves and exclaves, it had remained substantially the same shape for over a thousand years until the boundary changes of 1974, when the Vale of White Horse was taken over from Berkshire. Here we shall be concerned only with the old county, as it was before 1974.

The Oxfordshire countryside is without extremes, an unspectacular landscape of flat plains and gentle hills, of woods, cornfields, meadows and slow-flowing streams; yet it contains much variety. It straddles the geological grain of the country, with successive bands of different rocks forming alternating uplands and vales. The strata are generally inclined south-eastwards, so the hills tend to present a steep scarp face towards the north-west with a much gentler slope towards the south-east. The uplands in the north and west are drained by three major tributaries of the Thames: the Windrush, coming down from the Cotswolds through Burford and Witney; the Evenlode, which enters the Thames near Eynsham; and the Cherwell, which rises in Northamptonshire and flows through Banbury to meet the Thames at Oxford. Two further tributaries drain the flat clay vales: the Ray, rising above Bicester and meandering sluggishly through the marshland of Otmoor to meet the Cherwell at Islip; and the River Thame draining the lowlands around the town of the same name and entering the Thames at Dorchester.

The oldest rocks in Oxfordshire, the Lower Lias Clays, outcrop only in limited areas in the north-west, in the upper Evenlode and Cherwell valleys. Overlying the clays, the Middle Lias Marlstone, more resistant to erosion, forms the broken, rolling countryside west of Deddington and Banbury, climbing to 226.5m (743 feet) above sea level at Shenlow and Epwell Hills near Edgehill. A multitude of springs seep out from the junction between the water-bearing marlstone and the impermeable clay, and the hills are dissected by numerous streams, mostly draining eastwards to the Cherwell. The highest ridge of these North Oxfordshire Uplands forms part of the main watershed of England, however, and west of Tadmarton Heath the streams drain towards the Bristol Channel. The marlstone provides rich, red, loamy soils traditionally regarded as the finest cereal land in the county. The warm, orange-brown building stone gives a distinctive character to all the local towns and villages. The older cottages here were traditionally thatched.

South of Deddington we enter another upland belt formed by the Oolitic Limestones, which extend across central north Oxfordshire from the Cotswold Hills to Mixbury on the Buckinghamshire border. In the west the Oolites form bare upland plateaux with thin, brashy soils, rising to 247m (810 feet) above sea level near Little Rollright. Dry stone walls divide the fields. Although now predominantly arable, the Cotswolds were once renowned for their vast sheepwalks. The oolites provided some of the finest building stone in England, and these beautiful creamy-grey limestones are still the dominant material in the Cotswold towns and villages. At Stonesfield near Woodstock fissile beds within the oolite were mined and laid out to be split by winter frosts into thin slabs. Roofs of graded dark grey-brown Stonesfield Slates, often encrusted with moss, lichens and stonecrop, perfectly complement the limestone walls.

Part of the West Oxfordshire Cotswolds, between the Glyme, Evenlode and Windrush valleys, was covered in the Middle Ages by the great royal forest of Wychwood. Despite its antiquity, however, this was not a virgin wilderness; in the very deepest fastnesses of the woodland remains of prehistoric burial mounds and Roman villas show us that the land was once settled and farmed, only to be abandoned after the fifth century. Most of Wychwood has now once again been cleared and brought under cultivation, but around Charlbury, Woodstock and Witney many smaller oakwoods survive, fragmented remnants of the forest.

The lower slopes of the Oxfordshire Cotswolds are liberally sprinkled with magnificent mansions and splendid landscaped parks—Heythrop, Cornbury, Ditchley, and, grandest of all, Blenheim. Many of these parks originated as deer enclosures in the Middle Ages, but were later transformed by the activities of landscape gardeners. The concentration of parklands continues east of the Cherwell, with Bletchingdon, Kirtlington, Middleton Stoney, Shelswell and Tusmore; but here the limestone plateaux are lower, flatter, and more featureless, the fields more often divided by hedges than stone walls. Some of the streams in the north-east drain towards the Ouse, and so ultimately into the Wash.

Along the foot of the Cotswold dip slope there is a narrow but persistent band of Cornbrash, a shelly, rubbly limestone. On the north flank of Ot Moor this rises to the surface in a low, discontinuous ridge protruding above the Oxford Clay, providing dry sites for a string of villages from Oddington to Ambrosden.

The Oxford Clay, which underlies the broad lowland along the north bank of the Thames around Bampton and Eynsham, and continues north-east of Oxford into the Otmoor region, forms an ill-drained area of subdued relief. West of Oxford it is overlain by river terrace gravels, providing lighter, more fertile soils which, from the evidence of aerial photographs, have been intensively settled over thousands of years. North-east of Oxford the clay vale is lower and even flatter, drained by the sluggish River Ray, which was partly canalized in the nineteenth century to divert water away from the great marshland bowl of Ot Moor. Formerly a wild and remote region, Ot Moor has now been tamed by drainage and enclosure; yet even today a few portions still resemble the waterlogged morass of earlier centuries.

Another broken range of hills rises east of Oxford above the southern flank of Ot Moor. Many of the woods clothing these slopes are relics of the medieval royal forests of Shotover, Stowood and Bernwood. The Corallian Limestone, the main underlying rock, has been quarried for building, but some of its beds are very vulnerable to weathering, and this has left a legacy of problems for some of the Oxford colleges. The highest points on the ridge, including Muswell Hill (197m, 647 feet above sea level) and Shotover Hill (171m, 562 feet), are capped by more recent strata, including the Kimmeridge Clay, Portland Beds and Lower Greensand, which also form the lower rolling plateaux around Clifton Hampden, Nuneham Courtenay and Great Milton.

South-eastwards again the Gault Clay creates a broad vale between Thame and Dorchester. Because of the lack of building stone most of the older houses here are timber-framed with thatched roofs, and there are occasional examples of walling in cob, a mixture of mud and straw. Brick was also widely used from an early date. Above the Gault the Upper Greensand forms a slight, rather discontinuous step between Brightwell Baldwin and Postcombe.

The south-eastern tip of Oxfordshire straddles the chalk escarpment of the Chiltern Hills, which rise to 254.5m (835 feet) above sea level at Shirburn Hill. Numerous pure springs emerging along the Chiltern scarp foot have attracted a long string of villages from Ewelme to Chinnor. The dip slope, cut by many dry valleys such as Bix Bottom, is partly mantled by deposits of Clay-with-Flints. Here extensive beechwoods formerly supported a flourishing local furniture industry and other wood-using crafts. Chalk blocks have sometimes been employed for building in the Chilterns, but red and silver-grey brick and flint are more widely used.

Oxford, Beesley's osier yard in Upper Fisher Row above Hythe Bridge, c1880. Jacob Beesley, the proprietor, stands on the right by the fishing net, eel bucks and crayfish creels; he was an unusually large man, standing some 6 ft 3 in, and his family had worked as watermen and fishermen on the Thames for generations. The works provided seasonal employment for local women from April throughout the summer; here they are peeling bark from the osier rods after soaking them.

This is, then, a rich and varied landscape, well-endowed with natural resources, which has been lived in and exploited by man for many thousands of years.

Although occasional finds of flint handaxes from the Thames terraces around Oxford and the gravels beneath the Chilterns take the record of human activity back some 350,000 years, no evidence of local settlements appears until after the end of the Ice Age. As climatic conditions gradually improved the land was colonized first by sedges and grass, next by birch and aspen scrub, then pine and hazel, and finally, about 7000 BC, by mixed woodland dominated by oak, elm, alder and small-leaved lime. In the woodland small bands of people supported themselves by fishing, hunting and collecting berries and nuts. The distribution of their characteristic flint implements shows that by about 4500 BC man was ranging widely over the Cotswolds, the Corallian ridge, the Chilterns and the river valleys.

A little under 5000 years ago man began to effect more profound changes upon his environment. Woodland was cleared for grazing, primitive wheats and barley were cultivated, and more permanent settlements were established. Some of the archaeological sites dating from this neolithic (New Stone Age) period were substantial works, implying sizeable, stable populations with a considerable capacity for organization. Long barrows for communal burial are strikingly concentrated on the Cotswolds west of the Cherwell. Causewayed enclosures in the upper Thames valley, now only visible from the air, may have been seasonal gathering-places associated with the transhumance of livestock. Examples of *cursus*, enigmatic features of unknown purpose defined by parallel ditches up to a mile long, were laid out at Dorchester and Benson on the middle Thames. Later in the neolithic and early Bronze Age henge monuments, large circular religious enclosures defined by a ditch and external bank, were constructed at Stanton Harcourt and Dorchester (both now destroyed). The Devil's Quoits stone circle was subsequently erected within the Stanton Harcourt henge. On the North Oxfordshire uplands the Rollright Stones, comprising the Whispering Knights chambered tomb and the King's Men stone circle, are the most striking monuments of this period.

Round barrows signal the arrival of people using bronze tools and weaponry. Extant barrows are again largely confined to the Cotswolds, but aerial photography has shown that many others which once existed on the valley gravels have since been levelled by intensive later cultivation. Little is known of their contemporary settlements, although some enclosed hilltop sites such as Chastleton Camp may originate in the late Bronze Age (c1050–800 BC).

Iron implements begin to appear around 800 BC. Population growth intensified competition for land resources, and the emergence of a more warlike society is reflected by the building of earthen-ramparted forts on many of the higher hills. Small enclosures like Lyneham and Chastleton were superseded by larger, more formidable hillforts like Madmarston, which probably served as local administrative and market centres as well as providing communal defences. Not all the people lived in hillforts, however. A valley settlement at Standlake was excavated by Stephen Stone as long ago as 1857. Nearby, at Hardwick in the Windrush valley, archaeologists have excavated a pioneer pastoral farmstead first established around 220 BC. Another unenclosed farming settlement with circular huts was excavated at Milton Common before the construction of the M40 motorway. Crop marks on Oxford's Port Meadow suggest seasonal livestock grazing on the Thames floodplain. On the Cotswolds aerial photography has recorded examples of another distinctive class of site, the banjo enclosure, so-called from its long entrance droveway and roughly circular shape.

The old idea that hillforts were set in clearings overlooking an untamed wilderness of dense lowland forest can no longer be upheld. The whole landscape was now fully exploited. Wheat, barley and beans were widely grown on the gravel terraces. Sheep were pastured over the uplands. Cattle grazed the clay lowlands. Riverside meadows were mown for hay. Woodland, now greatly reduced in extent, provided acorns and beechmast for pigs, with large areas also regularly coppiced.

Towards the end of the millennium some hillforts were abandoned or reduced in importance as Belgic peoples moved into the region. New types of large defended lowland settlements now appeared, such as the Dyke Hills at Dorchester, where impressive earthworks span the promontory between the Rivers Thame and Thames; aerial photographs show the gravel spur within the Dykes to have been densely occupied. Another near-contemporary earthwork is Grim's Ditch in Wychwood, a territorial boundary enclosing some 14,080ha (22 square miles). A tribal society had emerged, with the present area of Oxfordshire lying on the frontiers of the Catuvellauni to the east, the Atrebates to the south and the Dobunni to the west.

The Roman annexation of the region between AD 43 and 47 was accomplished swiftly with little effective opposition, and any Roman military occupation was short-lived. New engineered roads such as Akeman Street were sliced through the landscape like a knife-cut, linked with a network of minor roads. No major Roman cities grew up in the Oxford region, reflecting its tribal frontier status before the occupation. Nonetheless, the small towns of Dorchester and Alchester must have had some official administrative status since they both acquired defences in the mid second century. Large undefended settlements at Chipping Norton, Swalcliffe Lea, Wilcote and Asthall probably served as local market centres. Over much of the countryside farmsteads and small villages continued a way of life little affected by Romanization; but on the lower slopes of the Cotswolds north of the Windrush there emerged a significant concentration of villas, whose occupants aspired to a more lavish life-style. The Northleigh and Stonesfield villas, in particular, had developed into sumptuous country houses with elaborate tessellated pavements and baths by the fourth century. Mixed farming was intensified, with new crops, such as flax and grape-vines, introduced. The Oolitic Limestone was already being quarried for building stone and roofing slates, and the clays around Oxford supported a pottery industry which, by the early fourth century, was a major production centre of Roman Britain.

The end of the Roman occupation was protracted rather than cataclysmic. The breakdown in the centralized administrative machinery is reflected archaeologically by the disappearance of coinage and pottery soon after AD 400. Early fifth-century pagan burials at Dorchester suggest that Anglo-Saxon mercenaries were recruited by the local communities to protect them in a time of increasing uncertainty and instability. Over the next few decades Anglo-Saxon peoples flooded into the region. Soon they had wrested political supremacy from the native authorities, except in the Chilterns, where an independent British enclave may have lingered on into the late sixth century. Early Saxon buildings appeared within the defences of Dorchester, at first respecting the Roman street alignments. Irregular hamlets with timber halls and sunken-floored or cellared huts, often only briefly occupied, also sprang up in the countryside: excavated examples include a sheep-farming settlement near Eynsham occupied until the early eighth century, and another Saxon hamlet near Cassington where the inhabitants lived by meat and dairy production and pottery-making.

In 571 the Anglo-Saxon Chronicle records a campaign in the Chilterns resulting in the West Saxon capture of Eynsham and Benson, marking the final consolidation of the Oxford region within the Kingdom of Wessex. The Old English language had now usurped the place of British speech, and, apart from a few river- and hill-names, provides the roots of most modern Oxfordshire place-names. The contrast in the distribution of certain common place-name elements reflects equally basic differences in the contemporary landscape: the ending -*tun* (usually modern -ton), indicating a settlement in open country, is widespread over Oxfordshire except in the Wychwood region and the Chilterns, whereas the element -*leah* (usually modern -ley or -leigh), meaning a woodland clearance, is strongly localized in those two areas. The woodland which had regenerated there since the end of the Roman period was now being colonized afresh.

Christianity came to Wessex in 635, when the missionary Birinus converted King Cynegils, who gave him Dorchester for his episcopal see. Within two decades this see had been moved to Winchester, and by 661 the upper Thames basin had been annexed by Penda, the vigorous pagan ruler of the midland kingdom of Mercia. The great barrow at Asthall, which contained a rich seventh-century Anglian cremation, is a monument of this short pagan revival. The power of Mercia was broken by the Danish incursions of the 870s, and subsequently Dorchester was re-established as a cathedral, this time as the centre of an immense diocese extending from the Thames to the Humber and the Wash. This endured till 1080, when the bishopric was transferred to Lincoln.

The spread of Christianity was accelerated by the foundation of minster churches served by communities of priests. St Kenelm's church, Minster Lovell, with its Anglo-Saxon dedication, represents one such site. Minster churches tended to be large and cruciform, and Bampton, Witney and Thame have retained this distinctive plan despite later rebuilding. Often they remained the centres of enormous parishes, with many dependent chapels. Smaller parish churches often began as private estate churches, and those at Asthall, Chastleton and North Aston stand right next-door to their manor house. The inhabitants of small hamlets remote from their parish church sometimes successfully petitioned to have their own chapel; these were usually small towerless buildings, such as Noke, built in the twelfth century within the bounds of the ancient parish of Islip.

Stonesfield Slate miners at the Rectory Drive pit in 1905: Jack Croxford, James Smith, Joseph Bumpus and John Smith, who were employed by Tom Barrett, the village shopkeeper. This was one of the deeper slate mines in Stonesfield: its main shaft was 66 ft deep, giving access to levels 3–5 ft high, and the stone was raised by hand windlass, then laid out in the fields nearby to be split by the winter frosts before its final shaping. Stonesfield slates are still seen on many roofs in west Oxfordshire.

It is no longer believed that most English villages owe their site and layout to the initial period of Anglo-Saxon settlement. It now seems more likely that the big nucleated village characteristic of most of Oxfordshire (apart from the Chilterns) did not develop until the late Saxon period; and it is quite clear that fundamental changes in village plans were still taking place throughout the Middle Ages, with some villages declining or disappearing, others expanding through organic or planned extensions over their own fields, and some being replanned with an entirely new layout. The reasons for the appearance of the large village are still not fully understood, but the development of the open-field system of farming with its emphasis on communal operations, the consolidation of the parochial system of churches, and the imposition of feudal authority after the Norman Conquest, must all be significant factors.

Town life revived only after the late ninth century, when Alfred the Great and Edward the Elder had restored the supremacy of Wessex after the Danish invasions. They planned a strategic network of regional defensive centres known as *burhs*. Instead of reutilizing Roman Dorchester as a *burh*, a new site some miles upstream, controlling an important ford over the Thames, was chosen. Here, near the old minster of St Frideswide, the new town of Oxford was founded, based on a cruciform street plan within a roughly rectangular enclosure of earthen defences. This piece of late Saxon town planning is still preserved in the shape of central Oxford today, with its four main streets meeting at Carfax.

After the Norman Conquest, King William saw fortified *burhs* like Oxford as a potential threat, so he built a strong castle immediately outside the Saxon western defences. Queen Matilda was besieged here through the bitter winter of 1141, eventually making her escape over the frozen Thames, clad in white to provide camouflage against the snow. Norman barons built further castles at Chipping Norton, Middleton Stoney, Deddington, Swerford and Ascott-under-

Wychwood. After the thirteenth century private castles could only be built by royal licence, and later examples such as Greys Court (1347), the moated Shirburn Castle (1377) and, finest of all, Broughton Castle (licensed in 1406) showed more concern with domestic comfort, fortification being comparatively minimal.

Much land belonged to the church. The Benedictine abbey established at Eynsham in 1009 flourished throughout the Middle Ages, but today only vestiges of its fishponds remain visible above ground. Three Benedictine nunneries were established in the twelfth century, the largest being Godstow, whose ruins may still be seen in the Thames-side meadows 3km (2 miles) north-west of Oxford. The wealthiest Oxfordshire monastery was the Augustinian abbey of Osney, of which only a few fragments survive in the western suburbs of Oxford. After the Dissolution Osney Abbey's church served briefly as the cathedral for the new diocese of Oxford, but four years later the see was moved to another former Augustinian priory which had been founded on the site of St Frideswide's minster in 1122. The nave of St Frideswide's was truncated in 1525 to make way for the quadrangle of Cardinal Wolsey's new college. After Wolsey's fall from grace his foundation was reconstituted as Christ Church, and the former priory church now serves a unique dual function as college chapel and diocesan cathedral. At Dorchester the ancient ecclesiastical tradition was carried on by another Augustinian abbey, founded in 1140, and here the church continues in parochial use.

Monasteries managed their lands through granges or estate farms. At Church Enstone the barn of the grange of Winchcombe Abbey (Gloucestershire) was built by Abbot Walter de Wynforton in 1382; another barn at Tadmarton belonged to Abingdon Abbey (Berkshire). Some Oxford colleges managed their estates in a similar way, and in the late fourteenth century New College built three splendid barns at Adderbury, Swalcliffe and Upper Heyford.

The twelfth and thirteenth centuries witnessed a further surge of town foundations. Early in the thirteenth century the Bishop of Lincoln laid out a new borough at Thame; here the vast cigar-shaped market-place, lined with ribbon-like burgage tenements, provides a classic example of medieval town planning. Similar evidence can be seen at Witney, Chipping Norton and Henley-on-Thames. Not all town promotions were successful, however: chartered boroughs at Middleton Stoney and Chinnor and markets at Hook Norton, Adderbury, Stratton Audley, Islip and Standlake failed to achieve lasting success, and these places are no more than villages today. Oxford remained the most important town, and when its commercial prosperity declined in the later Middle Ages, vacated properties were eagerly bought up by the colleges of the University, which had established itself there in about 1160.

During the Middle Ages much of Oxfordshire followed the midland style of open-field strip farming, and the characteristic pattern of broad, high-backed ridge and furrow, with its reversed-S shape reflecting the course of the plough along the individual strips, may still be seen on the claylands. The river floodplains provided hay, a commodity so highly valued that some upland villages maintained rights in distant meadows in the Thames valley: Northmoor, for example, belonged to the Cotswold manor of Taynton. In the Chilterns mixed farming predominated, with scattered open fields amongst enclosed land, common pasture and woodland.

Certain areas were legally reserved as royal forests, where the king could hunt. The largest and most important was Wychwood, but there were smaller forests east of Oxford. Although the king's forests were not continuous swathes of unbroken woodland, they did nonetheless include many woods to provide cover for game. Deer were also kept in parks surrounded by a high bank topped by a paling fence or wall, with an internal ditch to prevent escapes. Remains of the king's park at Woodstock were later incorporated into the eighteenth-century park of Blenheim. Beckley Park was broken up for farmland in the Tudor period, but the curved outline of its boundary can still be traced amongst the fields. Medieval parks were maintained primarily to provide rough woodland cover and grazing for deer. Coppice woods, by contrast, were regularly cut for pole-wood and fuel, and grazing livestock had to be kept out after cropping so that the trees could sprout new growth; although such woods tend to have the same elliptical shape as parks, their surrounding banks have their ditch on the outer, rather than the inner side. Burleigh Wood near Bladon is a typical example, and there are many more in the Chilterns which, though extensively wooded, were never legally a forest.

Economic decline during the later Middle Ages resulted in almost a quarter of the villages in Oxfordshire becoming deserted, leaving many evocative sites like Hampton Gay, where the church stands isolated in the fields, surrounded only by low mounds and banks representing the vestiges of abandoned houses and gardens. The Black Death in 1349 wiped out a few villages which were never resettled, and more were destroyed by Tudor landlords evicting the villagers to enclose their strips for sheep-farming; but the most common cause of desertion was simply the piecemeal voluntary abandonment of holdings by tenants leaving to seek a better living elsewhere. As more land went down to pasture because of the depleted labour force, a new class of graziers and merchants grew rich by raising sheep and exporting wool. At Chipping Norton the wool merchant John Ashfield financed the rebuilding of the church nave in about 1485. The even more magnificent church of Burford similarly reflects the great prosperity resulting from the fifteenth-century Cotswold wool trade.

The Dissolution of the Monasteries gave some men the opportunity to acquire immense wealth through the seizure of church estates. Among them was Sir John Williams, sheep grazier and High Sheriff of Oxfordshire, whose resplendent tomb dominates the chancel of Thame church. Under Mary Tudor, Williams was responsible for overseeing the burning at the stake of the Oxford Martyrs, Bishops Latimer and Ridley and Archbishop Cranmer, and the supervision of Princess Elizabeth's imprisonment at Woodstock Manor. His great mansion at Rycote is largely destroyed, but his plum-coloured brick lodge still stands in Beckley Park. Surplus wealth was now poured into more elaborate private houses and benefactions such as schools and almshouses. Early examples of the new classical Renaissance styles include the Jacobean mansion at Chastleton, built in 1603–12 by Walter Jones, a wealthy Witney wool merchant, and Wroxton Abbey, built for Sir William Pope. The ultimate expression of grandeur in domestic building was the vast baroque palace of Blenheim, begun in 1705 for John Churchill, first Duke of Marlborough, as an expression of gratitude from Queen Anne and the nation for his victory over the French.

Parks were now being designed as part of the setting of the great house. Up to the early eighteenth century formal layouts with long straight avenues and canals were fashionable, and Blenheim and Shotover still retain important features from this phase. In the 1730s a reaction against this formal tradition was begun by William Kent, who redesigned the small park at Rousham in the romantic or picturesque style, with meandering walks leading through a series of contrived views towards follies and statues. On a much grander scale the naturalistic remodelling of Blenheim carried out by 'Capability' Brown in the 1760s involved the planting of circular clumps and screens of beech trees and the drowning of the valley under a magnificent lake. Park design was now so important that sometimes entire villages would be swept away to improve the landscape. At Nuneham Courtenay Lord Harcourt demolished all the cottages near his mansion in 1760 and replaced them with a new estate village of neat brick cottages a mile away on the edge of the park.

Agricultural improvements, including the reorganization of the open fields and the introduction of new crops such as sainfoin, vetches and clover, gathered momentum during the seventeenth century. The most important change was the spread of enclosure. In Marston tenants and freeholders reached agreement amongst themselves in 1655 to enclose their entire parish. However, such agreements could be difficult to achieve, and a new procedure for enclosure by private Act of Parliament was first used in Oxfordshire at Salford on the Cotswolds in 1696. Most Parliamentary enclosures occurred between 1750 and 1875, the last at Crowell, on the edge of the Chilterns, in 1882. Through this procedure thousands of acres of open land were divided up into rectilinear closes with new hawthorn hedges, a staggering transformation. Enclosure of common grazing land threatened the livelihood of many smallholders, and was sometimes vigorously opposed. The inhabitants of the Ot Moor villages carried out a particularly energetic, though ultimately doomed, campaign between 1786 and 1835, chasing the surveyors off the moor, and going out by night with blackened faces to rip up the new hedges. Events reached a climax on 6 September 1830, when forty offenders were arrested and carted in towards Oxford prison; but this happened to be one of the days of St Giles' Fair, and sympathizers in the crowd pelted the guards with stones and effected a dramatic rescue. A more peaceful, but equally profound, transformation was wrought in Wychwood, where 2000 acres of forest were cleared and enclosed in 1856–7, and seven new farms built amongst the newly created fields.

The climate of agricultural improvement and industrial expansion demanded improvements in the transport system. Turnpike Trusts were set up to levy tolls upon travellers to finance road repairs. The Stokenchurch–Enstone road was the first in Oxfordshire to be turnpiked, in 1718, and by the beginning of Victoria's reign the network had spread all over the county. Stagecoach services took full advantage of the improved road surfaces, and coaching inns appeared along many of the main roads. The River Thames had been partly navigable throughout the Middle Ages, but it was obstructed by mills and fish-weirs, and in 1623 a Commission set up to improve the passage between Oxford and Burcot built the first pound-locks. Improvements continued, with new navigation cuts made at Culham in 1809 and Clifton Hampden in 1822. A wholly artificial new waterway, the Oxford Canal, authorized in 1769 and completed in 1790, linked Oxford and Banbury with the industrial West Midlands. Commercial traffic on the canals was ultimately killed by the railways. The main Bristol line of the Great Western Railway, built in 1840–41, was the first to penetrate Oxfordshire, crossing to the north bank of the Thames for three miles near Goring. Oxford was linked to the GWR by a branch in 1844, and by the end of the century a web of lines had spread out all over the county.

Industrial expansion was closely linked with transport improvements. Many of Oxfordshire's traditional industries are rooted in the resources and requirements of the countryside. The textile trades of several local towns can be seen as direct descendants of the medieval Cotswold wool trade. Blankets were made in Witney by hand-loom weavers in the seventeenth century, and cheap coal brought in by railway enabled power looms to be set up in factories. Tweed manufacture was commenced in Chipping Norton by Thomas Bliss in 1746. Banbury had several firms making horse-cloths and plush in the early nineteenth century. Leather tanning was also widespread, with glove-making being centred in Woodstock at least since 1580. Locally grown barley supplied a malting and brewing trade, and breweries are still working today in Oxford, Henley and Hook Norton. Agricultural engineering developed in Banbury in the nineteenth century. The demands of the University Press in Oxford resulted in a number of paper-mills being established, the last survivors being at Wolvercote and Sandford.

The present century has seen a massive acceleration in the pace of change. Traditional industries have declined, new ones have arrived. In 1913 William Morris built his first motor car in Oxford, heralding its transformation from a quiet university and market town to the modern bustling industrial city. The Thames valley around Stanton Harcourt and Dorchester has been scarred by sand and gravel extraction, devastating the important archaeological sites. Changes in agriculture since the last war have seen the decline of the small farm, the redundancy of traditional farm buildings, and the destruction of hedgerows. Changes in forestry practice have resulted in the spread of conifer plantations. Changes in social structure have caused the decline and, in some cases, destruction of the great country house. The savage contraction of the railway network since the 1950s has been counterbalanced by improvements in the road system, with the M40 motorway gouged through the Chiltern scarp, and bypasses relieving the congestion of many towns. Airfields have sprawled hideously over the flat lands of Brize Norton and Heyford. The extent of built-up land has exploded, with new towns like Carterton and Berinsfield, vast expansion in villages like Kidlington, and suburban growth around the towns. Successive editions of the Ordnance Survey provide graphic evidence of the profound changes which have been wrought in the Oxfordshire landscape since the nineteenth century.

Windsor Castle from the Park at the turn of the century. The castle, Berkshire's best known monument, has changed little since it was completed in stone in 1250. It was originally built of wood in 1070 in the shape of a motte with two baileys on land belonging to the Clewer Manor. It first became a royal residence in 1110 when it replaced the palace built by Edward the Confessor at Old Windsor. Today Windsor is among the first five tourist towns in the country with St George's Chapel and the royal apartments in the castle visited by many hundreds of people every day.

Berkshire

NLIKE MANY OF THE HOME COUNTIES Berkshire does not derive its name from the principal or county town, as do Oxford, Buckingham, Bedford and Hertford. The name is said to come from the Anglo-Saxon word *Berroc*, meaning a wood, although the Domesday Survey of 1086 does not indicate a heavily wooded shire. The name may derive from the Royal holding around Windsor where the forest, used by the Norman kings for recreational and hunting purposes, was quite extensive.

The shape of Berkshire, before the 1974 boundary changes, was always likened to a football boot, with Windsor situated on the toe cap to the east, and Oxford just across the border at its northernmost extremity. These two towns are linked by the River Thames which formed the northern boundary of the county, and continued from Oxford to its source near Lechlade, leaving Berkshire at Buscot. As one might have expected, the early historic and important towns of Reading, Wallingford and Abingdon were all situated on this waterway, which provided a means of communication and gave access to London.

The western boundary partly follows the route of the River Cole from Buscot to Shrivenham and then crosses the downs from Ashbury to Hungerford and Inkpen. From here the southern border follows no apparant natural features as it passes over the Eocene sands as far as Sandhurst, where it turns south-eastwards on the short stretch back to Windsor. To the north the county abuts Buckinghamshire and Oxfordshire, to the west Wiltshire, and to the south Hampshire and Surrey. Most of the east joins Bucks., but if one stands on Runnymede, where King John signed the Magna Carta, the counties of Buckinghamshire, Middlesex and Surrey can all be seen within the space of one mile.

The scenery in Berkshire, though perhaps unspectacular, is nevertheless very attractive, with many sleepy villages nestling among the rolling downs and river valleys. In contrast to these are the larger towns, all steeped in history, and mostly situated on major waterways. From early times the type of settlement within the county has been determined by the basic geology and topography of the different areas. Apart from the more recent alluvium which has built up in the main river valleys, the solid geology is much more ancient and comprises Jurassic, Cretaceous and Eocene rock bands which run parallel from the west to the east of the county.

The oldest of the series are the Jurassic rocks which occur at the very north of the county at the top of the boot. The first band, rising above the alluvium of the River Thames, is of Oxford Clay and stretches from Buscot and Eaton Hastings across to North Hinksey. Below this is the Corallian Ridge, a calcareous formation with hard limestone running from the Cole to the Thames and embracing Shrivenham, Coleshill, Faringdon, Stanford and Cumnor. The Vale of the White Horse, a natural valley carved out by the River Ock, separates the Corallian layer from a three-mile-wide band of Kimeridge Clay which contains shales and nodules of limestone. The villages of Goosey, Radley, Denchworth and Drayton stand on this as well as the town of Abingdon.

From here we move on to a series of Cretaceous rocks beginning with a band of Gault, which underlies the settlements of Wanborough, Uffington, Steventon, the Wittenhams and Didcot. A small outcrop of Lower Greensand, occurring in the area around Faringdon, is reported to be of special interest to geologists, and yields a large number of fossils. A band of Upper Greensand, not more than two miles wide, runs across from Wantage to Wallingford. The last but by no means least of the Cretaceous series is the Chalk, which covers at least a third of the county and forms the basis of the Berkshire Downs west of Reading. In the west it reaches from Wantage across the Lambourn Downs to Hungerford and the River Kennet. From west to east it stretches from Lambourn to Pangbourne with a narrow strip running into Reading. In east Berkshire the Chalk is represented by the southern end of the Chiltern Hills and covers the area from Twyford to Maidenhead and Cookham with an isolated knoll on which Windsor Castle stands.

The final third of the county is made up of later Eocene clays and sands. A narrow band of London Clay stretches from Inkpen in the extreme west right across Berkshire to Bray in the east. Despite its width, which in some places is only one mile, it encompasses the towns of Reading and Newbury, together with Thatcham, Tilehurst and Wargrave. London clay was used extensively for brick manufacture and all these centres have produced bricks and tiles at one time or another. The rest of the county to the Hampshire and Surrey borders is a mixture of Reading beds and Bagshot sands, the latter being an acid soil agriculturally unsuitable but producing areas of heather, gorse, silver birch and rhododendron. The towns of Wokingham and Bracknell are situated on these Eocene layers together with Windsor Great Park and Ascot.

Apart from the River Thames which flows along the northern perimeter of the county, there are other waterways, some of which provide drainage for the upland areas. The Kennet, which enters from Wiltshire, passes through Hungerford and Newbury before meeting the Thames at Reading. The River Lambourn starts in the downs, passes through the town after which it is named, and joins the Kennet at Shaw, near Newbury. The Loddon, which enters from Hampshire, crosses the county in a north-easterly direction through Twyford and into the Thames at Wargrave. Joining the Loddon near Swallowfield is the Blackwater which has a watershed south of Reading, whilst the River Pang crosses through the east downs before joining the Thames at Pangbourne. At the western end of the downs the Ock runs through the Vale of the White Horse from Shrivenham via Uffington to Abingdon where it meets the Thames, and the Cole flows into the same river at Lechlade.

Berkshire has always maintained an intermediate position between

London and Bristol, and most main lines of communication crossing the county tend to link these two cities. The earliest is the Roman road, completed not long after the conquest in AD43, and known locally as the Devil's Highway. After crossing the Thames at Staines (Pontes) it follows the southern border of the county through Crowthorne and Riseley on its way to the Roman town at Silchester (Calleva Atrebatum), a mile over the border in Hampshire. From here the route runs to Speen (Spinae) and across into Wiltshire on its way to the spa at Bath (Aquae Sulis), from where it linked with Bristol. The building of a road bridge across the Thames at Maidenhead in the thirteenth century eventually led to the formation of the Bath Road, which replaced the old Roman route. During the coaching era this was one of the busiest roads in England, passing through Reading, Newbury and Hungerford before entering Wiltshire. The opening of the Kennet & Avon Canal in 1811 provided yet another link, and water transport was used extensively for heavy loads until it was superseded by Brunel's railway in 1839. After negotiating the Thames at Maidenhead with his famous brick-built bridge, Brunel completed the Great Western Railway to Bristol in under a year. The final link came in 1970 when the M4 Motorway crossed the county like a spinal cord, bypassing the main towns and reducing traffic congestion in many areas.

The first settlers in Berkshire were attracted by the gravels of the River Thames and its tributaries. These were the hunter-gatherers of the paleolithic or Old Stone Age period who evolved sometime after one million years BC and continued, with minor cultural changes, until about 8000 BC. There is little to show of the dwellings of these nomadic people who hunted animals for their skin and meat, and gathered fruit and nuts to supplement their diet. Archaeological finds are confined to their hand axes and flint tools which are found on the gravel terraces of the rivers, mainly on the Thames or the Loddon. Such terraces exist up to 120 feet above the present river levels and were formed during the Ice Ages when rivers flowed alternatively slow and fast according to fluctuations in glacial conditions. Finds of hand axes tend to be confined to the east of the county at sites in Reading and Tilehurst, with large quantities at Furze Platt and Boyn Hill in the Maidenhead area. So prolific were the finds around Maidenhead that the Thames terraces, e.g. Boyn Hill, Furze Platt, Taplow and Winter Hill, were named after sites in the vicinity, even though these terms are used to describe terraces situated along the full length of the river.

About 8000 BC the hunter-fishermen of the mesolithic or Middle Stone Age came on to the scene. The change in climatic conditions had resulted in a new range of flora and fauna, and the people of this new culture moved nearer to the river's edge and added fish to their diet. The earlier large hand axes were replaced by the smaller Thames pick and an assemblage of flint microliths began to emerge. These were hafted to make arrows for hunting or spears to kill fish, and are found in many thousands on sites where they occur. The main area for evidence of this culture is the Kennet Valley where radio-carbon dates for settlement ranges from 8415 BC at Thatcham to 3310 BC at Wawcott. At Holyport, in east Berkshire, a large site was excavated on Shaffelmoor Stream, a tributary of the Thames, and yielded an assemblage similar to the Maglemosian settlement at Thatcham.

The first farmers of the neolithic or New Stone Age appeared in Berkshire by 3500 BC. They cleared areas of woodland to plant their cereal crops of wheat, emmer and spelt, and were the first settlers to move away from the river valleys. In many counties the chalk uplands were considered favourable for neolithic agriculture, but in the Berkshire Downs this does not seem to have been the case, unless evidence of settlement still awaits discovery. Pottery was introduced for the first time as were communal burial mounds in the form of long barrows. These only occur in the west of the county, the best known being Wayland's Smithy, which is situated on the Berkshire Ridgeway near Ashbury, and consists of a passage grave and façade constructed of sarsen stone from the Marlborough Downs. This example is the most westerly of the megalithic tombs of the Severn-Cotswold group, and other Berkshire long barrows, including Lambourn, which yielded a radio-carbon date of 3415 BC, appear to have had wooden chambers which were covered with earth and turves.

The other major type of monument that occurs is the so-called causewayed camp, which consists of a circular earthwork with ditches broken up by causeways at intervals. Their usage is not yet fully understood but they are thought to have been seasonal enclosures for pasturing animals, rather than a fortification or a place of ritual. One Berkshire example was found at Abingdon, and there are other unproven sites on the gravels of the Thames Valley.

Most evidence of neolithic occupation is to be found in the multi-period sites which occur in the river valleys. Finds vary from polished axes and items of antler or bone to the sagging round-based pottery so typical of the period. Evidence from the gravel plains appear to suggest that some of the early cultures may well overlap, and radio-carbon dates of 3320 BC, for a neolithic site at Canon Hill, Bray, and 3310 BC for a Mesolithic site at Wawcott appear to indicate this.

The people of the Bronze Age brought the knowledge of metal working to Berkshire around 2000 BC. Use of the river valleys continued with farmsteads and small settlements of wooden dwellings sited on the gravel plateaux. Bronze axes and other metal objects of this culture have been recovered from these settlements and on the river bed. The chalk downlands became the popular site for the funerary monuments of this period and some 140 round barrows have been located in this area. These burial mounds, replacing the earlier long barrows, are circular in shape, and come in many varieties, some of which have a surrounding ditch. Most contain the remains of only one individual, which may be an inhumation or a cremation, contained in a pottery urn situated at the centre of the mound. The best known group is the so-called Seven Barrows at Lambourn, a cemetery which actually contains more than forty mounds. Another group is to be found on Mortimer Common in central Berkshire whilst the only remaining two in the east are on Cockmarsh, a common near Cookham.

The Berkshire Ridgeway, a prehistoric route which extends from Streatley across the Downs into Wiltshire, may have come into use during the Bronze Age. If not, then it was certainly an established way by 500 BC at the beginning of the Iron Age. A series of large hillforts dating from this period are sited along the route. These forts, most of which cover several acres, were surrounded by up to three banks and ditches, and were believed to have been used seasonally or in times of seige. There are good examples of these which can still be seen at Uffington Castle, Blewburton, Little Wittenham and Caesar's Camp, Finchampstead.

Iron Age farmsteads and settlements occur in all valleys throughout the county, and there is good evidence for agricultural land use of the downlands. Celtic field systems with lynchets (ploughing ridges) have been detected in large areas of the west, mainly through aerial photography as subsequent cultivation has in many cases obliterated earlier evidence.

In the later Iron Age, around 100 BC, east Berkshire was affected by an invasion of the Belgae, a tribe from western Europe. They were responsible for the introduction of the potter's wheel and metal coinage to Britain, and increased trading with the Continent. With a town or *oppidum* established in Hertfordshire, they eventually crossed the Thames in the east and left evidence of their settlement in that part of the county. Robin Hood's Arbour, an animal enclosure on Maidenhead Thicket, and a settlement site at Star Works, Knowl Hill, both yielded sherds of their distinctive wheel made pottery, together with Roman imports which could be dated between AD 1–43, just before the Roman invasion.

Evidence of Romano-British occupation of Berkshire is very extensive and covers most of the county. There are, however, no sizeable Roman towns and those that exist in the area are tantalizingly situated just across the border. These include Staines, Dorchester-on-Thames, Mildenhall and Silchester. The last named was the cantonal capital of Calleva Atrebatum, which was the equivalent of an early county town for Berkshire although now it is situated one mile into Hampshire. There is no doubt that most of the county was governed from Calleva and that dues and taxes were paid to the administrators there. All major Roman roads in Berkshire lead to Silchester, the most important being the aforementioned Devil's Highway which linked the town with Staines and London. In a westerly direction a road led from Silchester to Speen, from where it divided into Ermine Street, which passed below Lambourn on its way to Cirencester, and the road to Bath via Hungerford. Another route went northward across the county to Dorchester, and there is considerable evidence to suggest that there was a major road linking Calleva to Verulamium (St Albans), passing through Waltham and leaving the county at Cookham.

During the Romano-British period Berkshire was very much an agricultural area mainly producing cereals to feed the army. Villa-farms were scattered over the whole county with the most substantial buildings in the east or close to the Thames. Even then the buildings, although sometimes large, did not compare with villas in other areas, and there were very few that had mosaic floors. The excavated villa at Cox Green, Maidenhead, is typical and shows a progression from a rectangular hall of the first century AD to a winged-corridor building with bath house in the fourth century, indicating an advance in prosperity. In the area to the east of Reading villas have been shown to be laid out in a triangular pattern at a distance of one and half miles apart, whilst in the downs they are less regular and tend to be a lot less substantial. Apart from an octagonal temple excavated at Waltham

St Lawrence, few other types of Roman buildings have been found within the county.

It was from the sixth century AD, in the Anglo-Saxon period, that documentary evidence first became available, and most of the major settlements in the county began to take shape. Reading was first documented in 870 when the Danes wintered there and repulsed the attack of King Ethelred and his brother Alfred, and was mentioned again in 1006 when the Danes returned. Old Windsor was the site of a palace of Edward the Confessor and remained so until 1110 when Windsor Castle became the royal residence. The castle, built about 1070 for defence purposes, was erected on land belonging to Clewer Manor, and it was some time before the town of New Windsor grew up around it. Wantage is famed as the birthplace of King Alfred in 849, and the powerful Abbey of Abingdon was founded in 675 by Hean, a Wessex nobleman. Sonning was an important ecclesiastical centre at an early date, and White Waltham the centre of a royal estate. Cookham, situated on the border of Wessex and Mercia, had a monastery by 750 and was the site of a meeting of King Ethelred's Council in 997. The Burghal Hideage of 919 mentions the fort of Sceaftesege at Sashes Island, Cookham.

Other Saxon settlements included Lambourn, Kintbury, Bucklebury, Thatcham and Aldermaston. The most important town, however, was Wallingford, which even today retains its ninth-century ramparts. In the Domesday Survey of 1086 Wallingford was the principal town in Berkshire, and one of the two boroughs mentioned, the other being Reading. Old Windsor must also have qualified for borough status, as the survey mentions the settlement as having ninety-five *hagae*, or house plots, a word normally only used in an urban context. Aldermaston and Thatcham also had a few houses and must be considered as proto-urban settlements.

The Domesday Book lists 192 manors in Berkshire of which only 21 are in the east, perhaps because of the large area taken up by the Royal

Forest at Windsor. The manors were held either by the king in lordship, the larger abbeys like Abingdon, or by tenants-in-chief who had been awarded land by William the Conqueror for their part in the Conquest. An analysis of the Domesday entries, however, shows that apart from the above-mentioned towns all the other manors were quite small and of a rural nature.

Reading had been a town since 1066, but took on a new importance after the abbey was founded in 1121 by Henry I. By 1205 there is a mention of a Guildhall, and by 1300 the town had a mayor and had become established as the county town. During the fifteenth and sixteenth centuries the population tripled, and there was a corresponding increase in manufacture and commerce. Meanwhile Wallingford had begun to decline in importance since the mid thirteenth century, and the diversion of the London-Gloucester road through Abingdon in 1416 hastened its demise. Abingdon remained under the control of the monks throughout the Middle Ages but lost its importance after the Dissolution.

By the twelfth century Old Windsor had lost its status, and a town was growing around the base of the castle at New Windsor. By 1268, in addition to a market and a fair, the town had a merchant guild. The castle was rebuilt and retained its importance as a royal residence.

During the Middle Ages new towns sprang up as market centres. Among these were Maidenhead, Newbury, Hungerford, Faringdon and Wokingham. Maidenhead began as a small settlement on the borders of Cookham and Bray, but grew in size when a road bridge was built across the Thames in about 1250, placing the town securely on the road to Bristol. Later this was to become the Bath Road, one of the busiest routes in the country. Newbury, situated on the Kennet, was mentioned as a borough in 1189, and expanded as a centre manufacturing wool and cloth during the sixteenth century. This town was also situated on the Bath Road, as was Hungerford, which became a borough in 1170 and had a market by 1296.

Faringdon, situated at the extreme north-west of the county, was mentioned in 1144 when a castle was built there. Its growth as a market centre seems to have been due to its position on the route from Wantage to Gloucester, and the fact that it was the only settlement of any size in an area of downland villages. Wokingham, despite its Saxon name, receives no mention until 1146 when a chapel was built there. At this time it was recorded as part of Sonning, and administered by the Bishop of Salisbury. The town remained a detached part of Wiltshire until as late as 1845, which is probably why it receives no mention in the Berkshire Domesday Book.

Bracknell, the other sizeable town within the county, developed from the adjoining parishes of Warfield and Winkfield. It grew as a community at the junction of two major roads through Windsor Great Park, but not to any extent until the eighteenth century. In 1949 it was designated as a site for a New Town, and now has a population of 50,000 and a large industrial area. Ascot, famed for the royal racecourse which was built in 1711 by Queen Anne, was once a bailiwick in Windsor Forest rented from the Crown.

Today, Berkshire is much narrower in shape having lost the north-western section, together with Abingdon, Wantage and Wallingford, to Oxfordshire. At the eastern end the county was extended to include Slough and Eton. With the railway and the M4 motorway as a spine it serves as a dormitory area for London, and with large housing estates being built in what is known as the M4 corridor, the towns of Maidenhead, Windsor, Bracknell, Wokingham and Reading are almost adjoined. This area is also being called 'Silicon Valley' from the industries that have grown up there. To the west of Reading the downland villages still retain their rural image, and remain unspoilt. The top tourist attractions in the county are Windsor, with its castle and safari park, and of course the River Thames, which apart from modernization, has changed very little since the first settlers came to Berkshire.

Map Section

Thame, the sheep market taking place in Upper High Street, 1897 (see page 86).

KEY TO ONE INCH MAPS

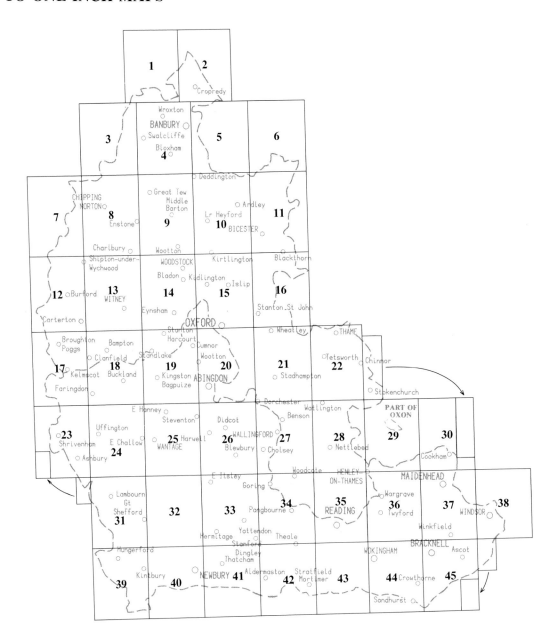

1

2

○ Cropredy

Wroxton ○
BANBURY ○
○ Swalcliffe

3

5

6

Bloxham
4 ○

○ Deddington

CHIPPING
NORTON ○

○ Great Tew
Middle
Barton

○ Ardley

7

8

9

Lr Heyford
10 ○ BICESTER

11

○ Enstone

○

Charlbury ○

Wootton ○

Shipton-under-
Wychwood

WOODSTOCK

Kirtlington ○

Blackthorn ○

12 ○ Burford
13
WITNEY

Bladon ○ Kidlington

Islip
15

16

14

○

Eynsham ○

Stanton St John ○

○ Carterton

OXFORD ○

Stanton
Harcourt

Wheatley ○

THAME

○ Broughton
Poggs

Bampton
○

Cumnor
○

Tetsworth ○

Chinnor

17

○ Clanfield

Standlake

Wootton

18

Kelmscot ○

19

20

21

22

Buckland

○ Kingston
Bagpuize

ABINGDON
○ □

○ Stadhampton

○ Stokenchurch

○ Faringdon
○

○ Dorchester
Watlington ○

PART OF
OXON

E Hanney ○

Steventon ○

Didcot

Benson ○

23

Uffington ○

○
WALLINGFORD

28

29

30

Shrivenham

E Challow
24

25 Harwell
WANTAGE

26

27

Nettlebed ○

Cookham ○

○ Ashbury

Blewbury ○
Cholsey ○

E Ilsley ○

Woodcote ○

HENLEY
ON-THAMES

MAIDENHEAD

○ Lambourn
Gt
Shefford

Goring ○

Wargrave ○

31

32

33

Pangbourne ○

34

35

36

37

WINDSOR

38

READING

Twyford ○

○

Yattendon
Theale

○

Winkfield ○

Hermitage

Stanford

WOKINGHAM ○

BRACKNELL

○ Hungerford
○

Dingley
Thatcham

○ Ascot

39

40

NEWBURY 41

42

43

44 Crowthorne

45

Kintbury ○

Aldermaston Stratfield
Mortimer

○ Sandhurst

Map 1

Map 1 The northern fringes of Oxfordshire occupy the marlstone plateaux behind Edge-hill and the Dassett ridge. The Hornton quarries were worked for building stone from the Middle Ages until their closure in 1924.

In the Domesday survey Mollington was divided between three counties, Oxfordshire, Warwickshire and Northamptonshire, and the Ordnance Survey 1st edition shows the boundary between Oxfordshire and War-wickshire still bisecting the village. Mollington was wholly taken into Oxfordshire in 1895.

Map 2 (overleaf) At the Three Shire Stones the northernmost tip of Oxfordshire meets War-wickshire and Northamptonshire. The Ox-ford Canal enters Oxfordshire nearby; begun near Coventry in 1769, construction had reached Banbury by 1778, and was completed through to Oxford in 1790. Claydon Lock is at the top of a series of five, the only flight of locks in Oxfordshire. Above it is the summit level of the canal, where the water-level was main-tained by several reservoirs, one of which is shown at Clattercote.

Map 2

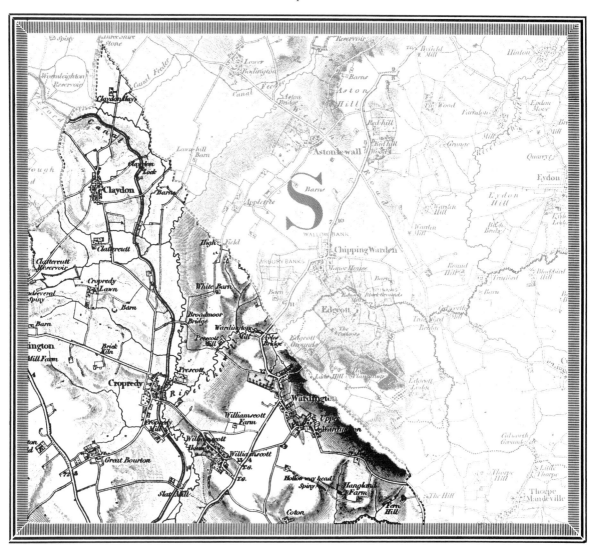

Map 2 cont.

The bridge at Cropredy was the scene of a battle on 29 June 1644, where the Parliamentarian forces of Sir William Waller were defeated by the King's army.

———◆◇◆———

Map 3 The north-western boundary of Oxfordshire follows the line of Ditchedge Lane, an ancient ridgeway along the crest of the marlstone uplands, which crosses the headwaters of the Stour at Traitors' Ford.

Shenington, formerly a detached part of Gloucestershire, was transferred to Oxfordshire in 1844.

Hook Norton is a large, sprawling village with numerous 'Ends'. At Scotland End, the only one named on the 1st edition, a brewery was established by John Harris in about 1850, using the abundant local springs; it has survived as an independent company and still operates today, though its present picturesque premises were not erected until the turn of the century.

Map 3

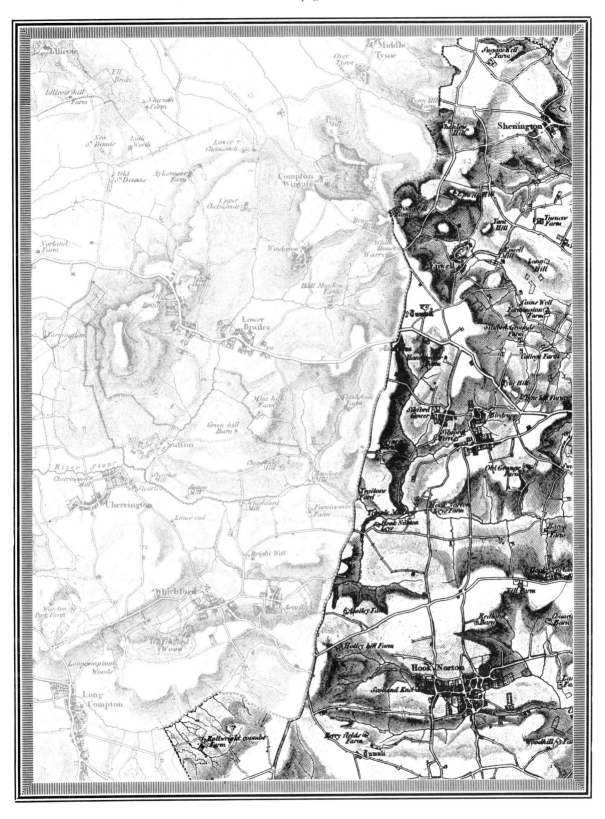

Map 4

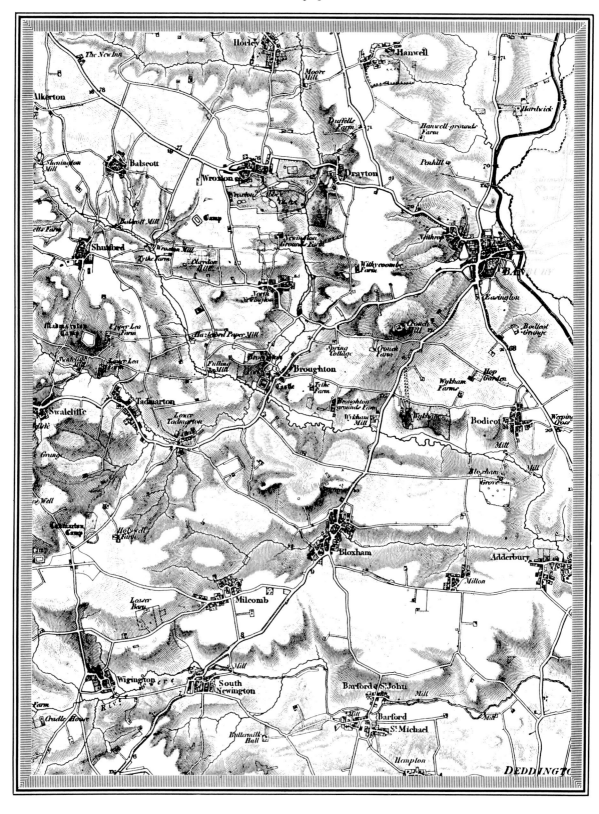

Map 3 cont.

East of Hook Norton the map shows orchards and farmland, but this area was to undergo drastic changes after the arrival of the Banbury & Cheltenham railway in 1887, through the large-scale quarrying of the marlstone for iron. The main line was carried over two great viaducts, extensive sidings and narrow-gauge quarry railways were laid out and four tall calcining kilns were built. This industrial phase lasted barely sixty years, however. The ironstone works and quarries shut down at the end of the Second World War, and the railway closed in 1962; most of the land was returned to agriculture and today only a few scars remain.

———————◇◆◇———————

Map 4 Several of the hills in the north Oxfordshire uplands are crowned with Iron Age earthworks. The most prominent of these is Madmarston Camp, where substantial ramparts were constructed late in the second century BC. This site was reoccupied in the late Roman period, and there was also a small Roman town in the valley around Lower Lea Farm. These early settlements may have served as markets and centres of local government before the rise of Banbury in the Saxon period.

Banbury was the centre of a large estate anciently belonging to the Bishops of Dorchester, and after 1072 to the Bishops of Lincoln. It was Bishop Alexander (1123–48) who built the castle and probably laid out a new market town there. We see it here just before its great industrial expansion following the establishment of Bernhard Samuelson's Britannia Engineering Works in about 1850; the manufacture of webbing, horse-cloths, plush, rope and furniture, along with brewing and

Banbury Cross in about 1880, seen from the north.

Present-day Banbury. The medieval High Cross was destroyed by the Puritans in about 1600, and the present cross was erected to commemorate the marriage of Victoria, Princess Royal, to Crown Prince Frederick of Prussia in 1858. Some townspeople objected to the raising of a religious symbol, others would have preferred a drinking fountain, and the resulting acrimonious arguments prevented the work being started before April 1859. Soon after its completion it was found necessary to surround it with lamps to stop people bumping into it on foggy nights.

Map 4 cont.

brick-making, were also important industries in the town. A hop garden supplying the local brewing trade is shown south of the town. The village of Shutford had been another centre of the plush industry since 1747, the last factory there closing in 1948. Numerous mills stand on the Sor Brook and its tributaries, including Hazleford Mill, which was already making paper before 1792, and Broughton Lower Mill, which was fulling cloth by 1685.

---◦◇◦---

Map 5 The River Cherwell forms the county boundary between Banbury and Clifton, its valley also followed by the Oxford Canal.

Adderbury is another large, sprawling north Oxfordshire village, which acquired the right to hold markets in 1218, though it never seriously rivalled Banbury or Deddington as a

Map 5

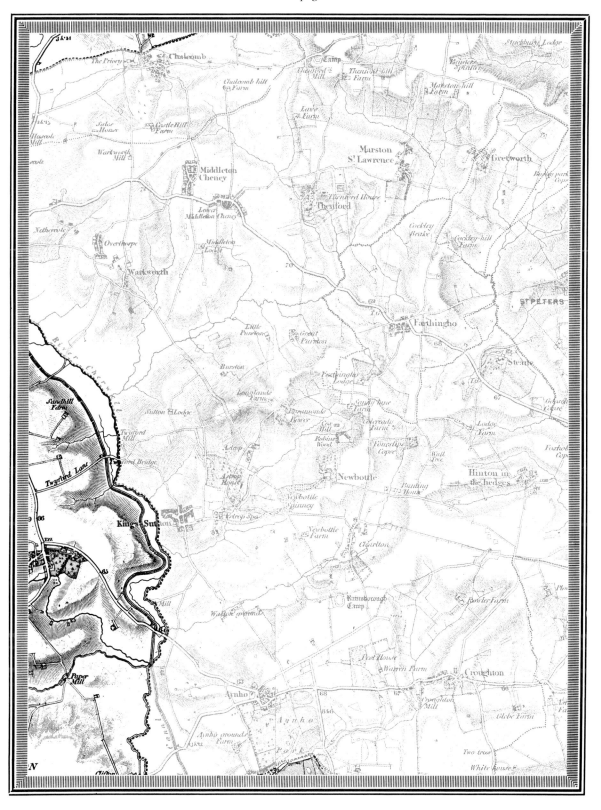

Map 6

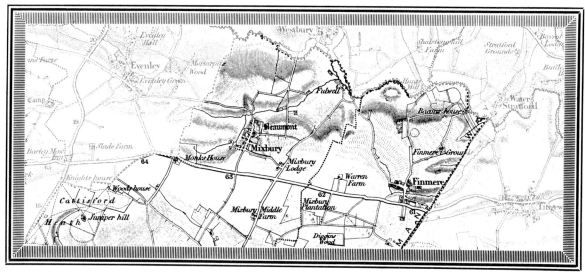

Map 5 cont.

local centre. The small park on the eastern side of Adderbury was landscaped by Capability Brown for the Duke of Buccleugh; its enlargement in 1768 is said to have caused the demolition of up to ninety cottages and the diversion of the Aynho road, thereby cutting off East End from the main part of the village.

The paper mill shown on the River Swere south of Adderbury was originally a corn mill, converted to paper-making in 1684 and finally ceasing work later in the nineteenth century; it has since been demolished.

———◇◇◇———

Map 6 The windswept plateau of Cottisford Heath still remained unenclosed in the 1830s. Like many other commons it was used for horse-racing in the early nineteenth century, with an annual meeting held at the end of the hunting season. The hamlet of Juniper Hill began with a couple of cottages built on the heath by the Cottisford parish authorities to house paupers in 1754. Cottagers established squatters' rights nearby, and farm labourers' dwellings were built there later in the nineteenth century. Life at Juniper Hill in the 1880s was vividly portrayed by Flora Thompson in *Lark Rise to Candleford*.

Beaumont in Mixbury was the site of the castle of Roger d'Ivry, the Domesday owner, though the existing earthworks are probably later. The present shape of Mixbury village differs somewhat from its depiction on the 1st edition, due to the demolition and replacement of many of the older cottages in 1874.

East of Finmere the county boundary follows the line of the Roman road from Alchester to Towcester.

———◇◇◇———

Map 7 At Chastleton a prong of Oxfordshire points out towards the Four Shire Stone, where it met Warwickshire, Gloucestershire and a former detached parish of Worcestershire. The present monument is eighteenth-century, but four boundary stones are recorded on this spot in a charter of AD 969. There are Early Iron Age hill-forts on Chastleton Hill and at Idbury.

At Churchill the old church, of which only the chancel survives, is shown isolated at the north-west end of the village. The village has moved away up the hill, and is served by a new church built in 1826, its tower a miniature copy of Magdalen College tower in Oxford.

Map 7

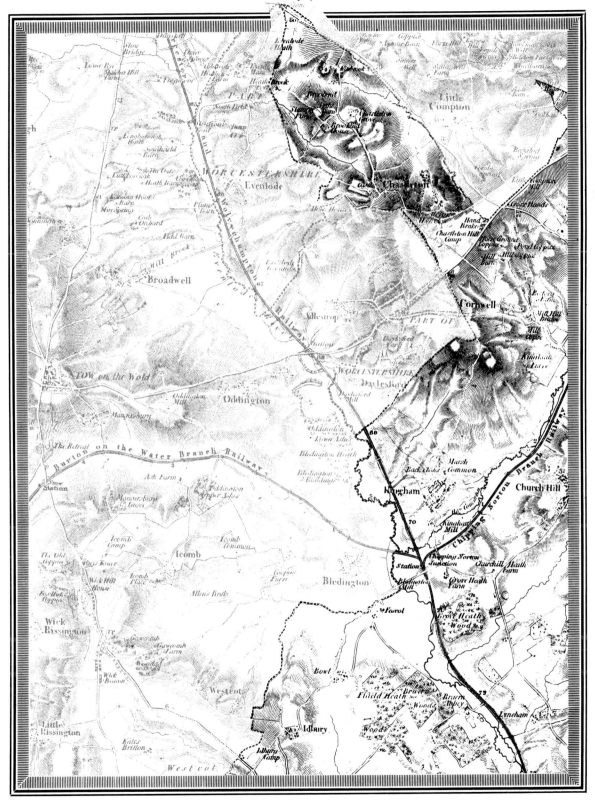

Map 8

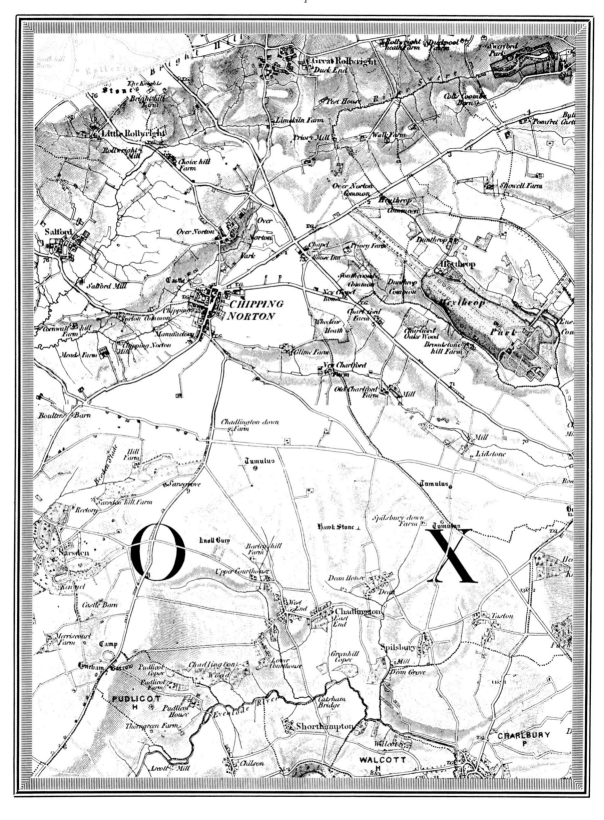

Map 7 cont.

Bruern Abbey is an early eighteenth-century baroque mansion built on the site of a twelfth-century Cistercian monastery, the foundation of which caused the destruction of the ancient village of Treton. The name 'Bruern' means 'heath', reflecting the wild and remote countryside in which the Cistercians frequently settled.

———◇◇◇———

Map 8 The West Oxfordshire Cotswolds contain many prehistoric sites, including the Hoar Stone at Enstone, the Hawk Stone at Chadlington, Knollbury Camp and the tumuli (barrows) on Chadlington and Spelsbury Downs. The most important group is the Rollright Stones, comprising the King's Men stone circle, an isolated standing stone known as the King Stone and a ruined burial chamber called the Whispering Knights or Five Knights. There is a rich folklore surrounding some of these sites, especially the Rollright Stones, which are said to be a king and his army turned to stone by a witch, the Whispering Knights being dissident members of his army who had drawn aside to plot against him. The stones of the circle are also said to be uncountable.

The upper Glyme Valley contains a number of deserted medieval hamlets such as Upper and Lower Chalford, probably abandoned in the fifteenth century. The surviving villages tend to be straggling, such as Enstone, divided into Church and Neat or Road Enstone, and Chadlington with its numerous Ends.

The rich farmland and pleasant character of the countryside tempted many wealthy men to establish country seats here, and there are large areas of parkland at Heythrop and Over Norton.

———◇◇◇———

Detail map 8 (overleaf) The principal town of north-west Oxfordshire is Chipping Norton, where the Fitzalans built a castle in the twelfth century and acquired market rights in 1205. Of the castle only earthworks remain, but the town still shows clear evidence of its planning in the Middle Ages. Its large rectangular market-place was later reduced in size by market stalls and shops and public buildings such as the Guildhall and Town Hall. On either side behind the buildings fronting the market-place the long, narrow yards resulting from the subdivision of the original regular medieval tenement plots can clearly be seen. In the fifteenth century the town prospered as a wool market, later developing a cloth industry, and in 1821 the firm of Bliss & Son began making tweed there. The manufactory shown on the Ordnance Survey 1st edition was supplemented in 1872 by a new mill in the valley to the west, designed with balustraded parapets to look like a great mansion in a park, and tweed-making continued on these premises until 1980. Brewing and glove-making were also important in Chipping Norton.

———◇◇◇———

Map 9 (overleaf) The concentration of big estates and parklands continues in the lower Glyme and Dorn valleys. Ditchley was acquired in 1580 by Sir Henry Lee, one of Elizabeth I's courtiers, and he retired here to create the first park in 1603, extended and altered in the eighteenth century. The park at Glympton was made in the 1630s, when the village was moved further away from the church and manor-house. The church of Great Tew is similarly isolated, part of the village having been removed by imparking before the late sixteenth century; at the time of the map the estate was held by the descendants of the Birmingham engineer Matthew Boulton, who were engaged in blocking and diverting further roads to enlarge the park, repairing and rebuilding cottages, and landscaping the whole to achieve a picturesque appearance.

There were strong social contrasts in the nineteenth century between closed estate

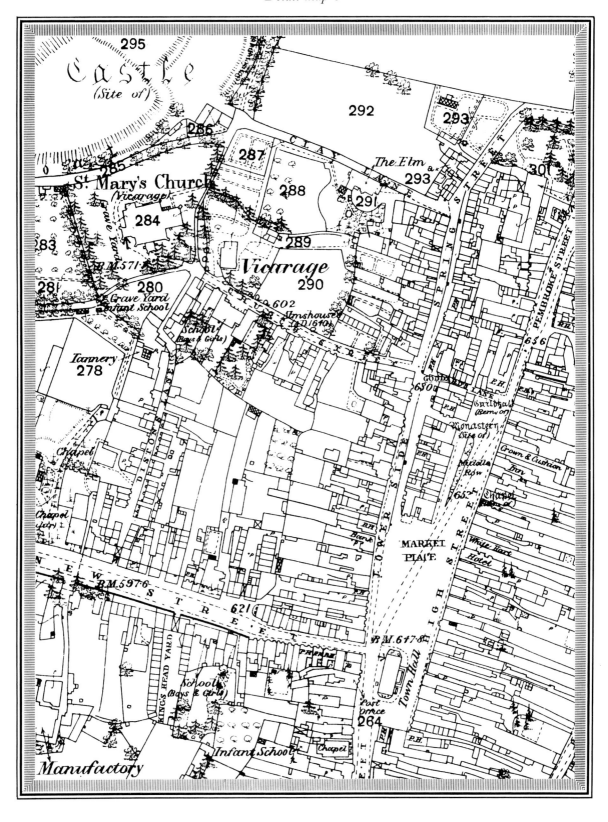

Map 9

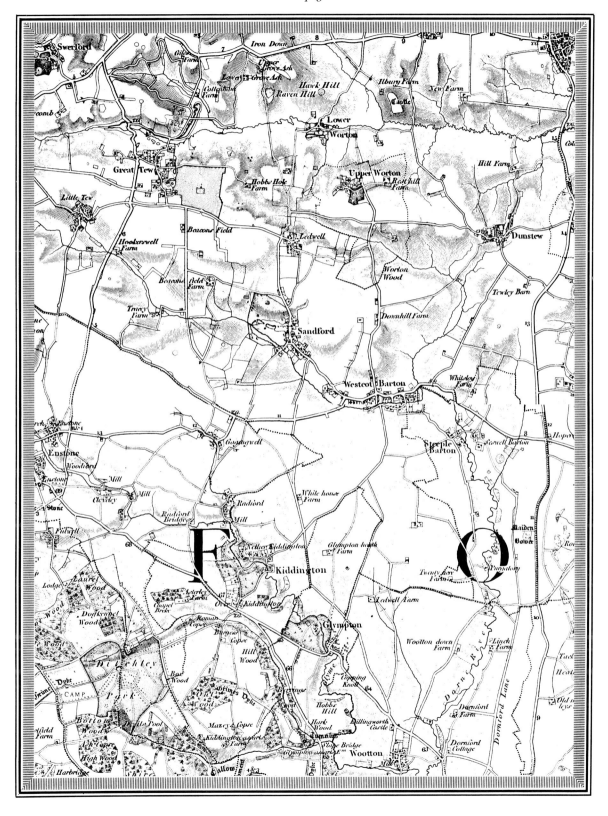

Map 10

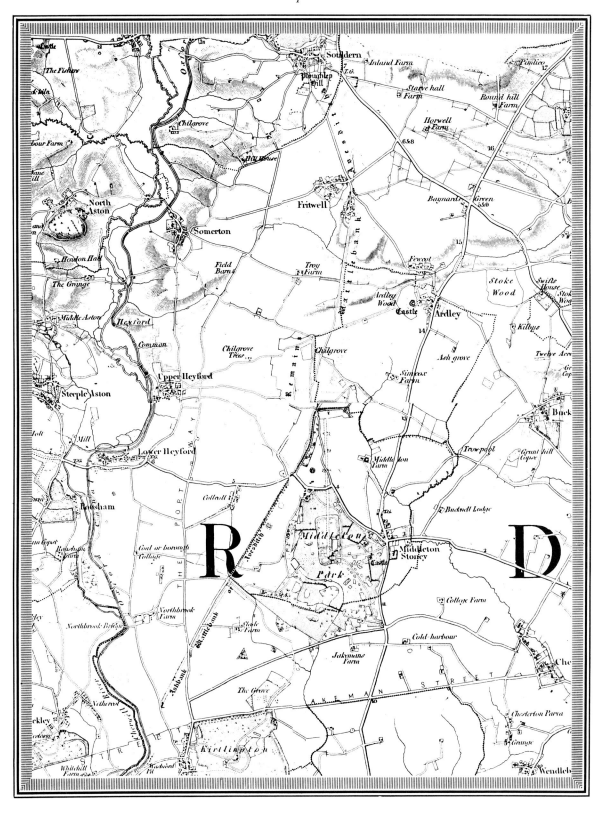

Map 9 cont.

villages strictly controlled by one big landowner, like Great Tew, Sandford St Martin or Steeple Barton, and open villages occupied by smallholders, tradesmen and labourers, such as Middle Barton, a sprawling, unplanned settlement east of the old centre of Westcott Barton, but still not yet separately named on the 1st edition.

Deddington is a decayed medieval market town which, by the mid-nineteenth century had no staple manufacture, its population being almost entirely employed in agriculture. Its castle was abandoned in the fourteenth century, and only earthworks remain.

———————◇◇◇———————

Map 10 Several ancient roads are shown east of the Cherwell, including the Roman Akeman Street, the earthwork variously known as Ash Bank, Wattle Bank or Aves Ditch, and the Port Way crossing what is now the US air base of Heyford. Ploughley Hill at Souldern was a prehistoric barrow used in Saxon times as a meeting-place for Ploughley Hundred.

The high density of parklands continues. Middleton Stoney was first enclosed in 1201, but the layout on the map is a product of later extensions, most recently in 1824–5 when the 5th Earl of Jersey removed the village and rebuilt it on the edge of the park. At Tusmore the park was created in 1358 after the village had been destroyed in the Black Death. From 1625 to 1806 it was the home of the Fermor family, amongst whom was Arabella, subject of Alexander Pope's *The Rape of the Lock*. The sharp dog-leg in the route of Akeman Street at Chesterton results from a diversion made in 1801 to allow George Clarke, the county sheriff, to enlarge the grounds of the Lodge.

Steeple Aston is another typical open village, which doubled its population during the first half of the nineteenth century, in contrast with Middle Aston, once the more populous place, but declining in population over the same period through the exclusive

policy of its sole owners, the Cottrell-Dormer family of Rousham.

———————◇◇◇———————

Map 11 (overleaf) Alchester was founded by the Romans on the marshes between two tributaries of the River Ray in the mid-first century AD. The Roman town was abandoned apparently in the fifth century, and in the Middle Ages its site lay under the open fields of Wendlebury, while Bicester emerged as the principal market centre of the region. The local supremacy of Bicester was briefly challenged by rival markets at Middleton Stoney (1279), Bignell (1377) and Stratton Audley (1318), but none of these enjoyed lasting success.

The only villages directly on the Roman road north-east from Alchester are Newton Morrell and Newton Purcell, whose names suggest that they were established comparatively late in the Saxon period. At Blackthorn the remains of its great rectangular green, enclosed in 1776, can still be seen. Cottisford and Fringford are the 'Fordlow' and 'Candleford Green' of Flora Thompson.

———————◇◇◇———————

Map 12 (overleaf) Further ancient enclaves of other counties show on this map: Shilton, part of the ancient Berkshire lordship of Faringdon, and Widford, historically in Gloucestershire because it belonged to St Oswald's Priory in Gloucester, were both transferred to Oxfordshire in 1844.

Much open field and unenclosed downland remains; Milton- and Shipton-under-Wychwood were finally to be enclosed in 1849 and 1852 respectively.

It is curious that the important Taynton quarries, which are recorded in the Domesday survey and were still being worked, are not shown on the map. Several paper mills are marked in the Windrush valley, including

Map 11

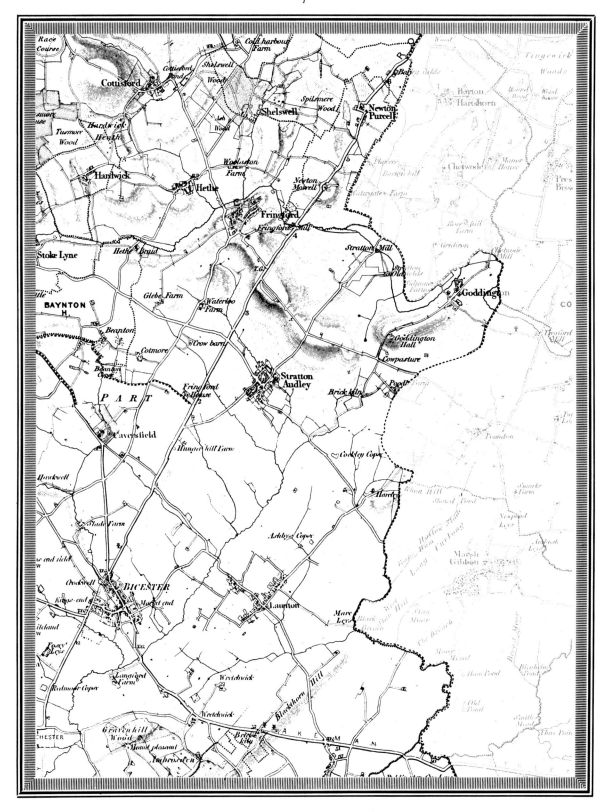

Map 12

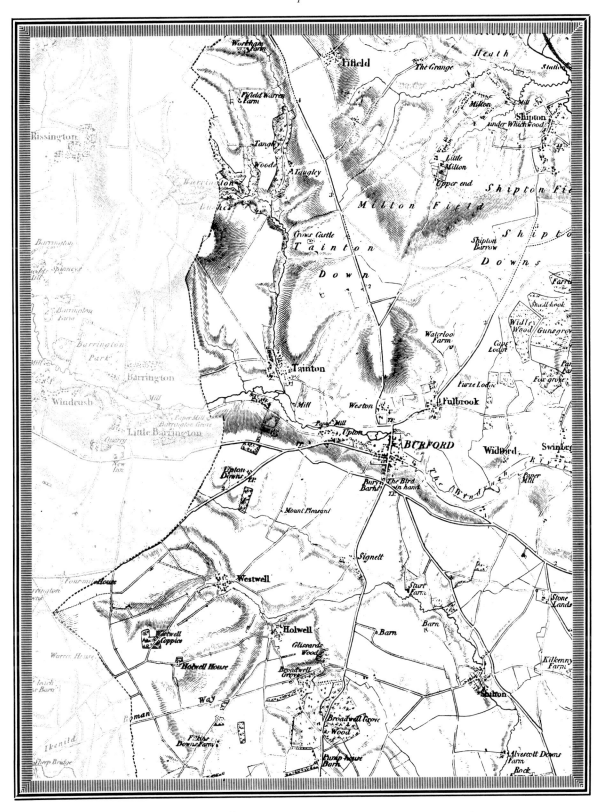

Upton and Widford, but these had closed before 1860.

Burford was the scene of a battle in AD 752 between King Cuthred of Wessex and King Aethelbald of Mercia, and its vast cruciform church contains evidence of its Saxon origins. The town prospered greatly from the wool trade, especially in the sixteenth century, and subsequently became an important coaching station. By the early nineteenth century, however, Burford was entering a period of decline; much traffic had been diverted along the top road past Bury Barn, newly turnpiked in 1812, where a new inn, the 'Bird in Hand', was built, and when the railways were built no line came within four miles of the town.

———◇◇◇———

Map 13 Considerable changes have taken place in this part of the Oxfordshire Cotswolds. In the early nineteenth century the

Forest of Wychwood still extended from the ancient royal deer park of Cornbury southwards and westwards almost to the Windrush, broken only by one large clearing containing the settlements of Leafield and Field Assarts.

There were two medieval market towns on the fringes of Wychwood. Charlbury was once a detached part of the Bishop of Dorchester's Banbury estate, where the bishop's north

Burford, the Michaelmas fair in the High Street, c1895. Burford once had several annual fairs, including a corn and cattle fair on the last Saturday in April, started in 1785; St John's fair, held in June at least since 1337, but discontinued in 1861; the main September fair for cheese, cattle and sheep originally granted by Henry VII in 1497; and a Mop, or hiring fair for servants and labourers held in Sheep Street, which ceased in 1914 (see also page 65).

Map 13

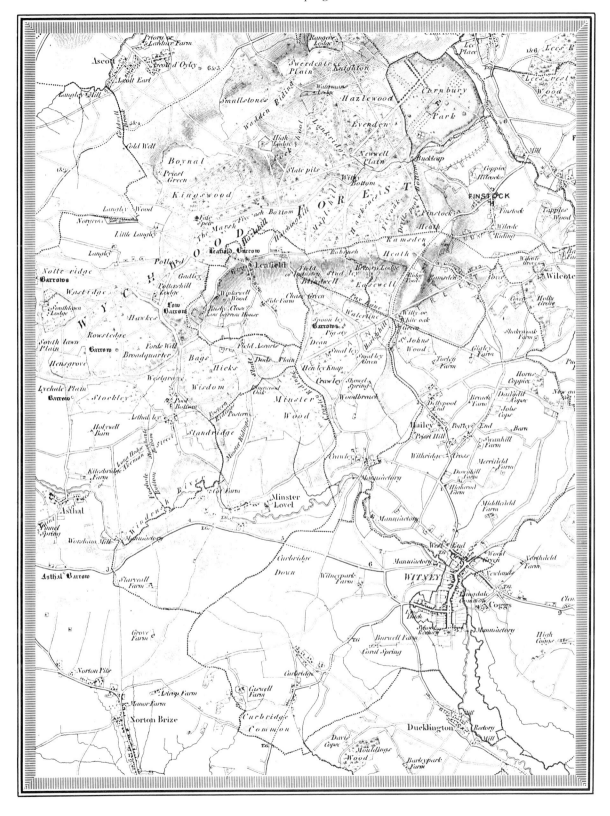

Map 13 cont.

Oxfordshire tenants had rights to collect wood and pasture their beasts in the forest. In 1094 it passed to the Abbey of Eynsham, which held it for the next 450 years and developed the town there. In the nineteenth century Charlbury had become a centre of the gloving industry. Witney was laid out as a new town in the early thirteenth century by the Bishop of Winchester, with a great wedge-shaped market-place (now Church Green). It had begun to specialize in the manufacture of blankets around 1600, and by the nineteenth century this was the staple trade of the town.

Modern map 13 By the middle of the nineteenth century Wychwood was a wilderness, its coppices overgrown and unprofitable, its pastures spoiled by uncontrolled overgrazing. Following an Act of Parliament, clearance began in 1856, and within fifteen months almost 2000 acres had been converted to farmland, only the north-eastern part towards Cornbury, and a few woods like Hensgrove, Stockley Copse and Priest Grove remaining. Ten miles of new roads were laid out amongst rectangular fields, and seven new farms were built; among them Chasewood Farm, with its three-sided windbreak of trees.

Mill Street, Witney, in 1987 (see also overleaf: hands going to work at Early's Blanket Mill in Mill Street, 1898). The cottages in the background were built to house mill workers. Woollen cloth had been woven in Witney at least since the twelfth century, and the specialization in blanket manufacture dates at least back to the seventeenth century. High-quality blankets were being exported to Portugal and Spain by 1768, and cheaper ones to North America.

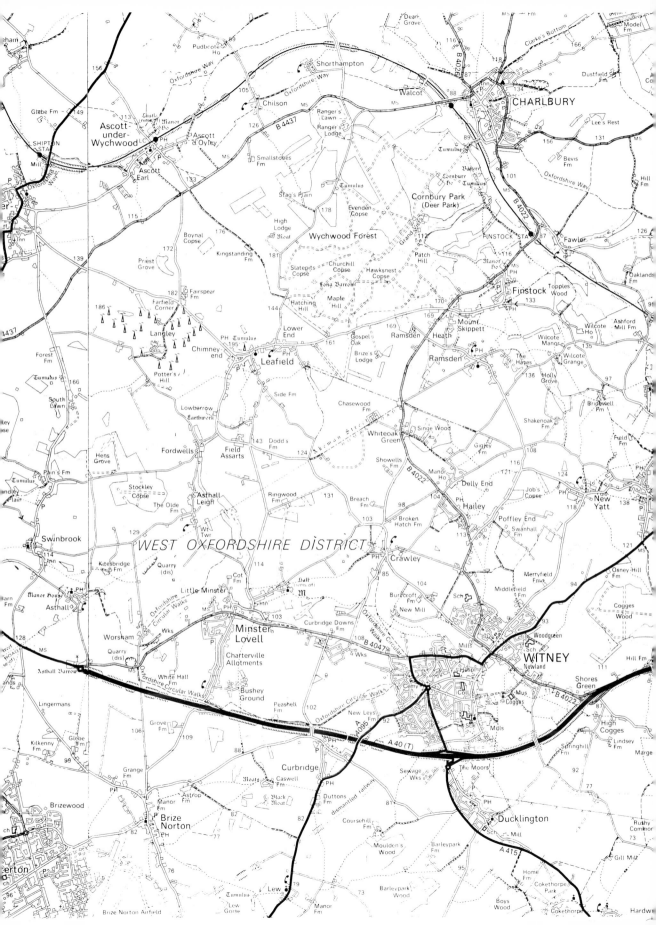

Map 14

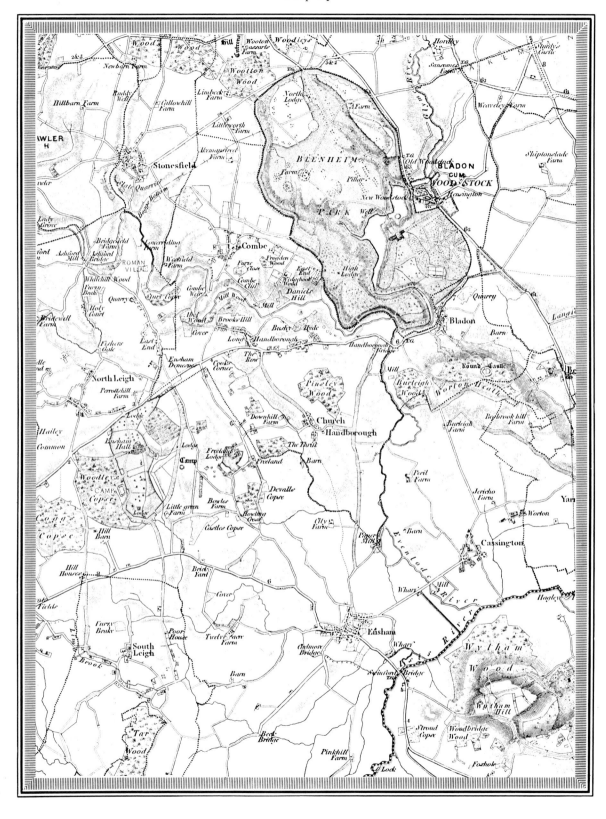

Burford High Street, once the scene of several annual fairs (see page 58).

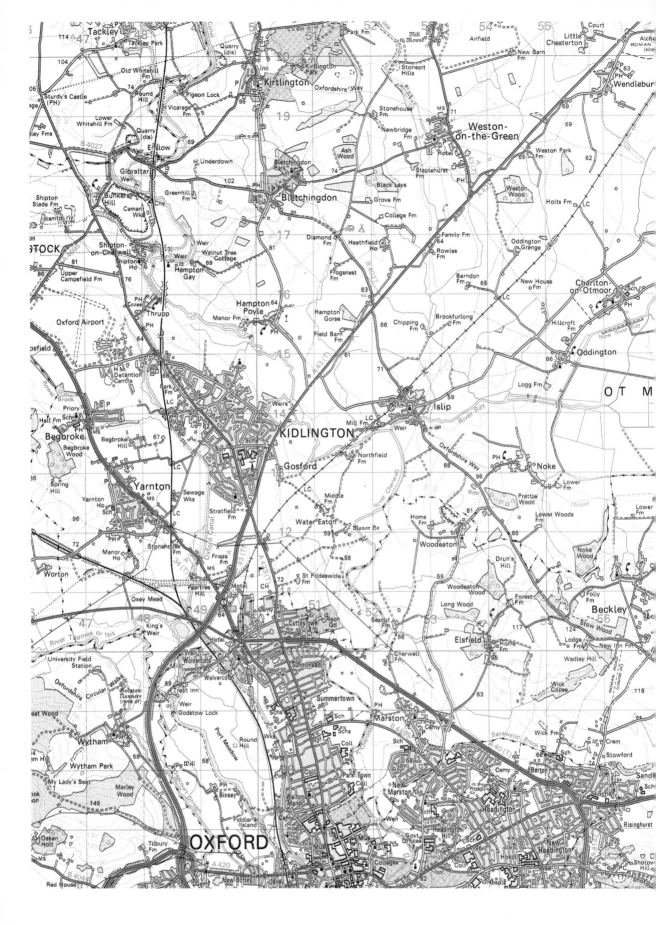

As the Wychwood hamlets expanded several acquired their own churches for the first time—Finstock in 1841, Leafield in 1860, Ramsden in 1872. A new hamlet appeared at Fordwells after 1861, to house labourers working on the new farms. Another new village was founded in the parish of Minster Lovell, where the Chartist Land Company, part of Feargus O'Connor's radical political movement, had acquired 300 acres of sheep pasture in 1847; this was broken up into seventy-eight smallholdings of two to four acres each and allocated to the winners of a lottery. Many of the original model cottages still survive in Charterville Allotments, though the distinctive character of the village has been lost through infilling.

Map 14 (page 64) The Roman villa by the Evenlode near North Leigh was discovered in 1813, excavated and is preserved for public view.

In the Anglo-Saxon period Eynsham (pronounced as it is spelt on the 1st edition, Ensham) appears to have been the main local centre. It was captured by King Cuthwulf of Wessex in 571, and in 1009 became the site of an important Benedictine abbey, which was responsible for the development of the little town outside its gates. By the middle of the nineteenth century Eynsham was entering a period of decline.

The small borough of Woodstock has a curious origin. King Henry II is said to have established his mistress, Rosamund de Clifford, in a bower in the park, spending so much time there that he found it necessary to purchase some waste land nearby to build accommodation for his courtiers and servants. In 1704 the royal park was granted to the 1st Duke of Marlborough, and Blenheim Palace was begun on the opposite bank of the river Glyme to the medieval hunting-lodge, facing 'Fair Rosamund's Well'. Later in the eigh-teenth century the park was landscaped with a new lake by 'Capability' Brown, but the 1st edition shows part of the older formal layout of circular glades and radiating avenues east of the palace. Woodstock was a centre of the gloving trade from the sixteenth century.

Stone roofing slates were mined at Stones-field at least since the seventeenth century, the last pit being abandoned only in 1909.

Map 15 (overleaf) The countryside im-mediately north of Oxford has undergone many changes. In the 1st edition Upper and Lower Wolvercote were still isolated villages at the north end of Port Meadow, the tract of common pasture which had belonged to the burgesses of Oxford since before the Norman Conquest. East of the Cherwell Marston and Headington were not yet engulfed by sub-urbanization. The northern fringes of the city had only just reached the University's Radcliffe Observatory, which had been built in open country after 1772. However, two detached developments already foreshadowed the later expansion of the north Oxford suburbs: 'The Terrace', now Park Town, a prestigious and exclusive estate built by a private trust in 1853–5, and 'Summerstown', now Summertown, where speculative de-velopments were springing up around the first house built amongst the cornfields in 1820 by a horse-dealer named James Lambourn.

The village of Wytham is at the northern extremity of Berkshire, and the land rises to 539 feet on Wytham Hill. The south side of the hill was part of Cumnor Wood which belonged to Abingdon Abbey as early as AD 955. The village is famous for its strawberries. The medieval nunnery at Godstow on the other side of the Thames is where Henry II's 'Fair Rosamund' was buried and where Agnes de Wytham was Abbess in 1415. The church is fourteenth-century but was rebuilt in 1811.

Map 15

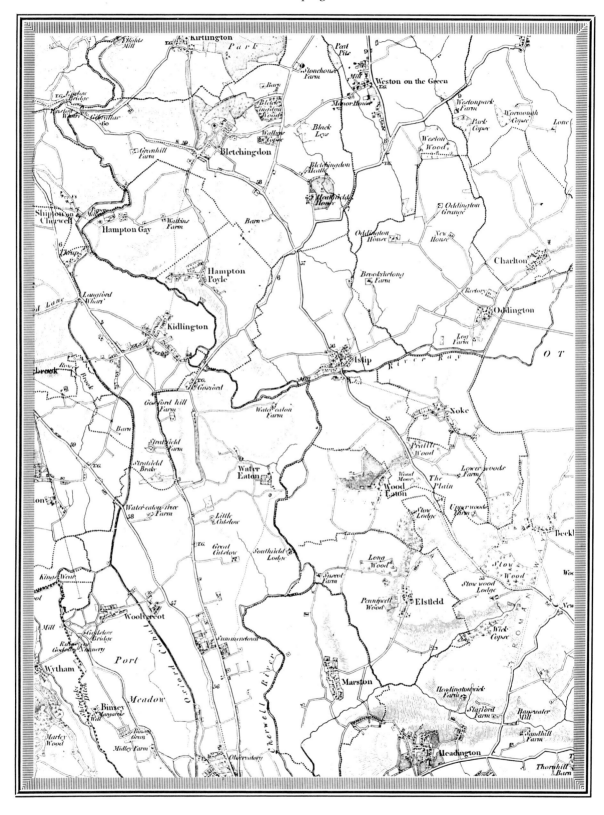

Modern map 15 (page 66) Two major changes have occurred since the mid-nineteenth century: communications improvements and enormous housing expansion.

Of the railways which began to radiate out from the town in the middle of the nineteenth century only the lines northwards to Banbury and Birmingham (opened in 1850), and north-westwards to Charlbury and Worcester (opened in 1853), still carry passenger traffic. Other lines were opened north-eastwards to Bicester and Bletchley (1851), and westwards to Witney (1861). Woodstock was served by a short branch leaving the Oxford–Banbury line at Shipton-on-Cherwell, opened in 1890 and closed in 1954. As the railways declined the road system was modernized, including the Oxford Northern Bypass built in 1935, the A421 Bicester road widened and straightened in 1938, and the Western Bypass built in 1961. At Kidlington the wartime airfield has developed into a commercial airport and pilot-training school.

The northerly expansion of Oxford was rapid. By 1900 housing had spread along the Banbury and Woodstock roads as far as Summertown, and by 1940 development had already breached the bypass cordon. East of the city Headington was engulfed by 1940, Old Marston by 1970. Kidlington grew rapidly through ribbon development in the 1930s, and other outlying villages like Yarnton have also developed as dormitory settlements.

———◇◇◇———

Map 16 (overleaf) On the eastern side of Ot Moor changes to the county boundary occurred in 1844 when Warren Farm and Whitecross Green in Studley were brought into Oxfordshire from Buckinghamshire.

In 1741 Sir Edward Turner, creator of Ambrosden Park, embarked upon a project to straighten the road from Ambrosden all the way into Oxford; however, as the map shows, he only managed to get as far as Merton.

Ambrosden House was pulled down in 1768.

The flat lands on the north side of Ot Moor contrast with the broken hills to the south, where some areas of woodland such as Studley, Waterperry, Holton and Stanton Woods survive from the Middle Ages. Beckley Lower Park is a moated Tudor brick house on the site of a medieval hunting-lodge. The isolated farm of Thumley (now Thomley), still a separate civil parish, occupies the site of a deserted medieval village.

Nether and Over Arncot appear as tiny, remote hamlets in the nineteenth century. In 1941 the War Office decided to site its Central Ordnance Depot here, and by 1954 this covered an area of over 3000ha (12 square miles).

———◇◇◇———

Map 17 (overleaf) In 1844 Little Faringdon and part of Langford were transferred to Oxfordshire from Berkshire. Among the attractions of this once quiet and remote part of the upper Thames valley are the Saxon church at Langford; the medieval bridge at Radcot, where on 20 December 1387 the Duke of Gloucester defeated the forces of Robert de Vere, Earl of Oxford and favourite of Richard II; and the Tudor manor-house at Kelmscott which was to become the retreat of William Morris after 1871.

About two miles south of Little Faringdon is the lock at Buscot, the second on the Thames after Lechlade. The village, bounded by the Thames and the Cole, has a twelfth-century church. The main part of the village was planned as a model settlement in 1897, and the area was a centre for agricultural experiment throughout the eighteenth century. The large house in Buscot Park was built in 1780 by Edward Loveden, who, amongst other things, improved the cheese trade in the area. Three thousand cheeses per year were despatched to London by barge from Buscot Wharf, many of which were made at Snowswick Farm in the parish. Eaton

Map 16

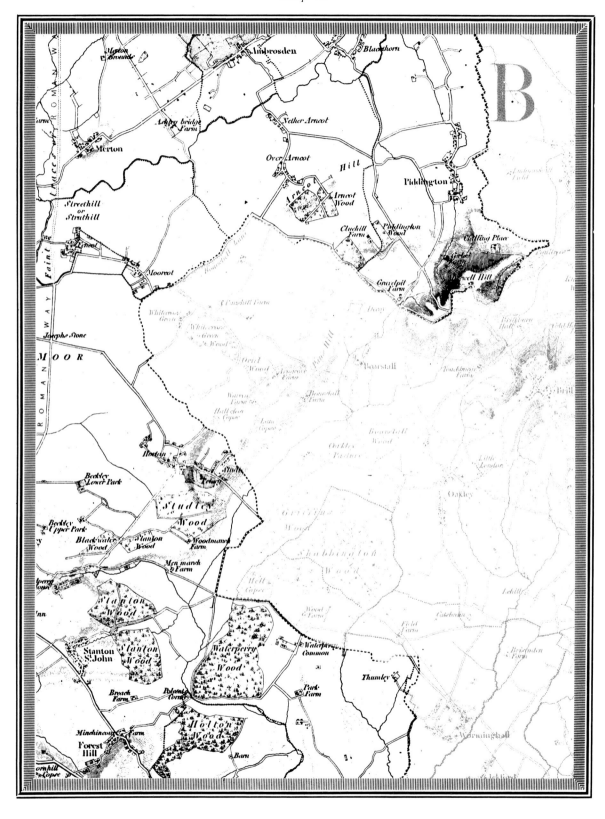

Map 17

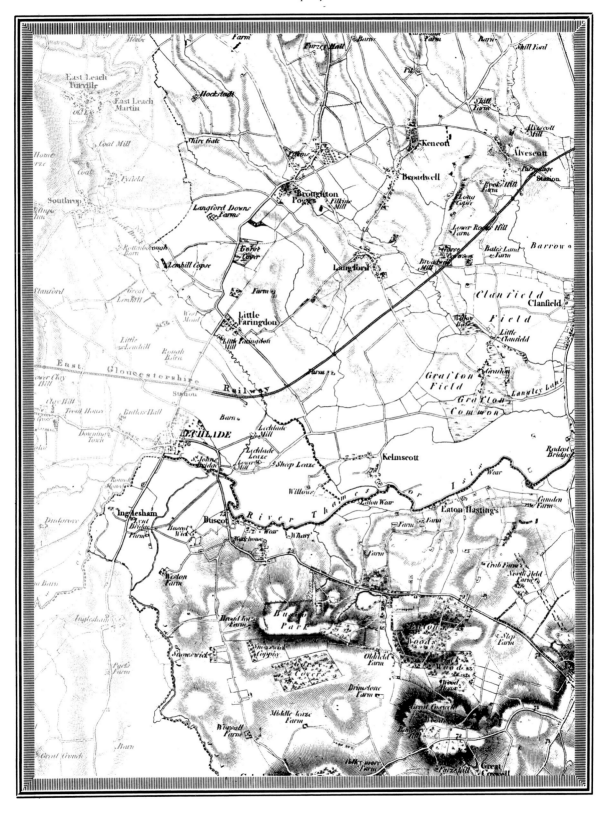

Map 17 cont.

Hastings, a little further along the Thames, is an attractive village with a mainly thirteenth-century church.

While the secluded atmosphere of this corner of Oxfordshire is not yet entirely destroyed, the modern world is pressing in from the north-west. In 1902 William Carter bought land near Rock Farm in Brize Norton from the Duke of Marlborough in order to establish a smallholders' colony. This was not a great success, but the establishment of RAF Brize Norton in the 1920s and its subsequent growth has provided sufficient local employment for Carterton to develop as a thriving new town.

Map 18 Faringdon, the largest settlement in the area, was the market town for western Berkshire. It is the only stone-built town within the county and has many interesting buildings. In the grounds of Faringdon House, which was built in 1780, a stone tower erected in 1936 stands on a hill known as Faringdon Folly, and is a landmark for miles around. The road to Abingdon passes through Buckland with its twelfth-century church. Buckland House, west of the village, was built in 1757 and has a deer park of 150 acres and a large lake. Hinton Waldridge, now Hinton Waldrist, has an Elizabethan manor house inside a moat and the remains of a Norman motte and

---

Sheep-washing in the upper Thames above Radcot Bridge, c1890. There has been a stone bridge here since the tenth century, but the present bridge, wide enough for two packhorses, was rebuilt in the fourteenth century (see page 84). Sheep-farming had been important in west Oxfordshire since the Middle Ages, and in the late nineteenth century much of the wool went to Witney for the blanket industry.

Map 18

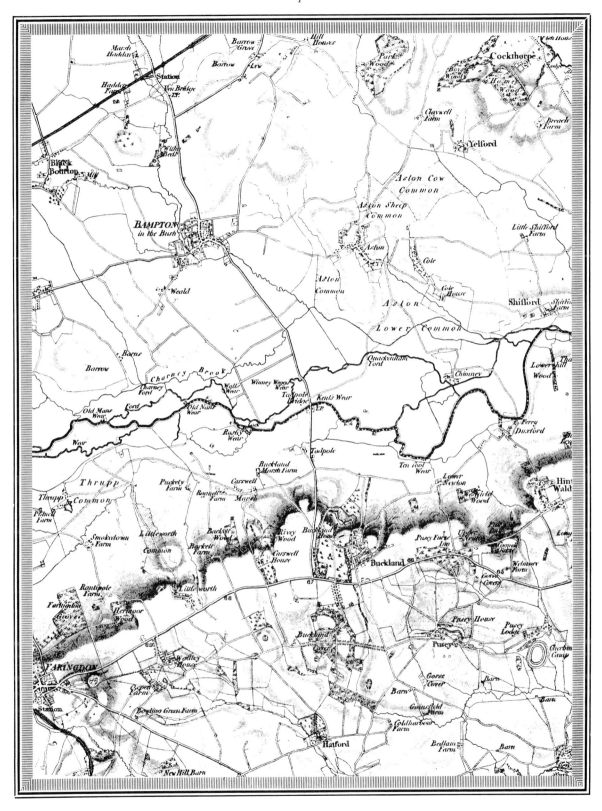

The buildings of Faringdon remain unchanged in this comparison of the scene in 1904 and that of the present. Where the sheep market was once held is now a through road designed to cope with modern traffic. Despite this, the town is a good example of a conservation area.

Map 18 cont.

bailey castle. Hatford (Herts), to the south, has an early manor house and church. Cherbury Camp is an Iron Age hillfort guarding the narrowest part between the Thames and the Ock, and legend has it that it was the site of a palace of Cnut, and was the camp which King Alfred visited in the guise of a minstrel.

Some six miles north of Faringdon the spire of the ancient minster church of Bampton is a landmark for miles around, and travellers could find the town readily enough; but before the late eighteenth century, when unsurfaced roads wandered amongst the surrounding common lands, finding their way out again was a different matter. On the 1st edition the town still bears its nickname 'Bampton-in-the-Bush', and though the wastes had been much reduced by enclosure the waterlogged lands around Aston were still common land. Bampton was an ancient royal estate and the centre of a vast parish; but by the nineteenth century its remoteness and inaccessibility were causing economic stagnation.

Great agricultural improvements were carried out through flood control measures in the 1850s, when William Wood cut a new drainage channel, the Great Brook, from Winney Wegg's Weir to Shifford. Improvements to the river navigation were also carried out, with a new cut short-circuiting the meander below Chimney made in 1896–8.

———◇◇◇———

Map 19 (overleaf) This area encompasses many villages between the Ock and the Thames. Cumnor is on land which belonged to Abingdon Abbey, and it is said that a hermit of Cumnor Wood selected the site of the Abbey. Appleton has a church built in 1200 and a moated manor house of the same date. Bessels Leigh is a Saxon settlement which belonged to Earmund in the seventh century.

The gravel terraces of the Thames around Stanton Harcourt and Standlake formerly contained many prehistoric, Roman and Saxon sites, of which the most important was the Devil's Quoits henge monument. Three standing stones survived until 1940, when the site was utilized for a wartime airfield. Since 1945 the whole area has been devastated by gravel-quarrying, and most of the archaeological sites have been destroyed or severely damaged.

Stanton, which takes its name from the stones, was the home of the Harcourt family from the twelfth century to the 1750s. Although most of their house was then demolished, the medieval kitchen, the gatehouse and the chapel tower where Alexander Pope translated Homer's *Iliad* remain.

Neither Standlake nor Northmoor are named in the Domesday survey, and their foundation is possibly associated with the renewed colonization of the Thames marshes in the early Middle Ages. Northmoor was a dependency of the distant Cotswold manor of Taynton. An extensive common remained south of Standlake until 1853.

Fyfield was first mentioned in AD 956 and has a fourteenth-century manor. Kingston Bagpuize, situated on an important crossroads, is a large parish with a Georgian mansion. Newbridge, to the north of the parish, is fifteenth-century and featured in the Civil War. Longworth House was built in the seventeenth century, and Charney Bassett Manor before 1300. Frilford is on a Saxon road from Wantage, and had a burial ground of that period at Noah's Ark. Marcham has thatched houses and a mill dating back to the Domesday survey.

———◇◇◇———

Map 20 (overleaf) Abingdon, although not mentioned as a settlement in the Domesday survey, was the site of the very powerful Abbey which was founded by Hean in AD 675. Lands held by the abbey extended across Berkshire, especially in the west. During the Middle Ages the urban community was under the control of the monks, but after the suppression in 1547 a

Map 19

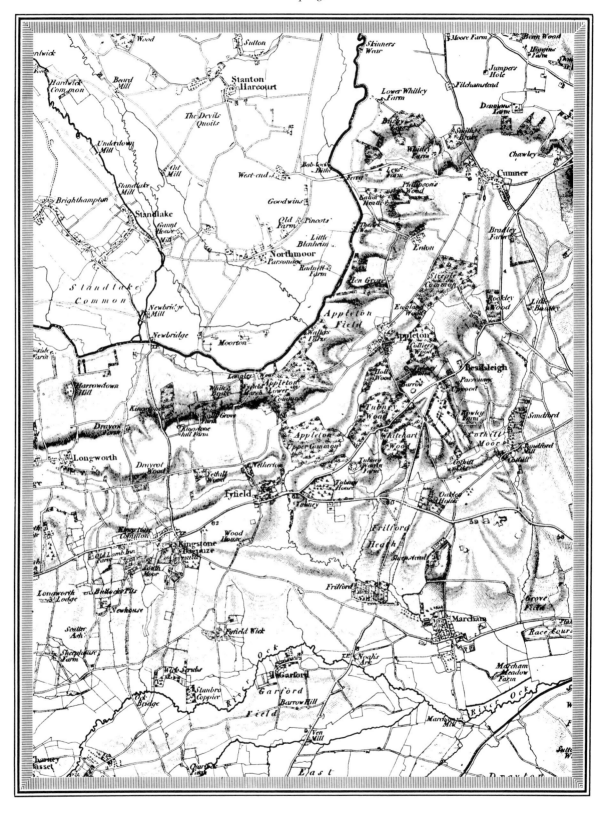

Map 20

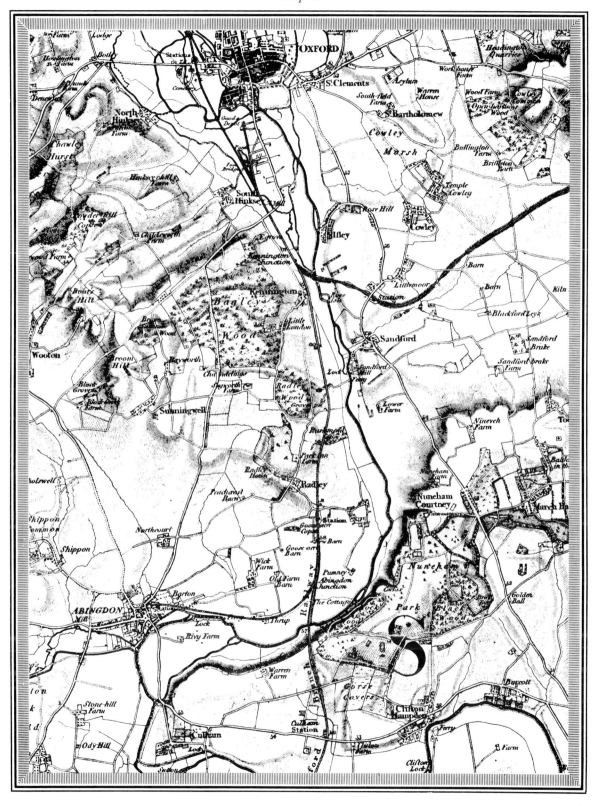

Ock Street, Abingdon, which leads from the town square to the river Ock, was mainly built in the eighteenth and nineteenth centuries, but the older buildings seem mainly to have been replaced when compared with the scene in c1895–9.

George Street, Oxford, from the west, 1903: the University dominated the eastern side of the city, but the western side was altogether less glamorous. All of the nearer houses on both sides of the street were swept away for redevelopment in the 1920s, and the City of Oxford Boys' High School, beneath the distant cupola, was closed in 1966, its buildings being taken over by the College of Further Education.

Oxford, the University quarter: view west up the High Street in the 1890s towards the distant spire of All Saints' Church (1706–08), with the New Quad front of Brasenose College (1886–9), the University Church of St Mary the Virgin (spire c1320, nave c1485–95, porch 1637) and the south front of All Souls' College (1826–7), with University College (1634–77) to the left. Apart from the intrusion of motor vehicles, this view is hardly changed today (see page 83).

Map 20 cont.

local government was set up. During the seventeenth and eighteenth centuries hemp, flax and malt were manufactured in the town. Abingdon still has many historic buildings, and excavations have revealed Saxon and medieval remains. Radley, to the north, is famous for its public school founded in 1847 at Radley Hall, a mansion erected in 1727. The church contains some fifteenth-century glass. Sunningwell was first mentioned in AD 821 and has an Elizabethan house at Beaulieu Court Farm. North Hinksey, on the banks of the Isis, had a ferry that dated back to 1467. South Hinksey in the Isis valley was the site of the reservoirs and waterworks which served Oxford.

The 1st edition shows that Oxford had still not spread much beyond its medieval walls,

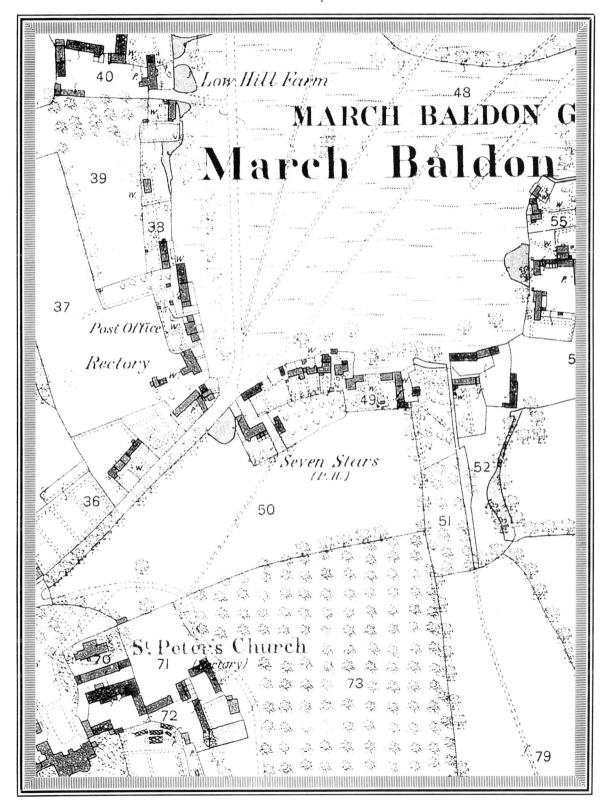

40

Low Hill Farm

48

MARCH BALDON G

March Baldon

39

55

38

37

Post Office

Rectory

49

52

Seven Stars
(P.H.)

50

51

36

S! Peter's Church

70   71   *(Rectory)*

73

72

79

Map 20 cont.

though the St Ebbe's and Friars districts to the south were built up and tentacles of development were beginning to spread westwards into Osney and eastwards into St Clement's. Iffley, Littlemore, Church Cowley and Temple Cowley were still separate villages, and the medieval hospital of St Bartholomew still stood in lonely isolation on the edge of Cowley Marsh. On the hills east of the city the Headington Quarries had been a source of building stone since about 1400, and a higgledy-piggledy scatter of quarrymen's cottages had sprung up there.

Below Oxford the Thames, after serving another paper-mill at Sandford, skirts Nuneham Park. In 1755 Simon, 1st Earl Harcourt, abandoned the old family home at Stanton Harcourt and built a new mansion at Nuneham, where the wooded slopes offered more potential for ornamental landscaping. The old village stood in the way of the improvements, and in 1760 Lord Harcourt swept it away and rebuilt it as two rows of neat brick cottages on the edge of the park. Oliver Goldsmith visited Nuneham in 1761, and it probably provided the inspiration for his poem *The Deserted Village*.

———◇◇◇———

Detail map 20 (page 81) Marsh Baldon has been selected to illustrate the detailed village plans found on the first edition of the Ordnance 25 inches to the mile series. Seven different estates called Daldendone are recorded in the Domesday Book, and in the thirteenth century there were villages at Marsh Baldon, Toot Baldon, Little Baldon and Baldon St Lawrence, of which only the first two survive today. The fact that all four Baldons shared the same field system in the Middle Ages indicates that they all at one time comprised a single estate. The low-lying, well-watered site of Marsh Baldon suggests that it may be a product of early medieval marshland colonization within the estate and the

nineteenth-century form of the name (March meaning a boundary), is misleading. The church of St Peter stands on slightly higher ground adjoining the seventeenth-century manor house; it was originally a chapel of Dorchester Abbey, and is first recorded in 1163. The main village surrounds a magnificent sub-rectangular green north-east of this older nucleus, some 9.7 ha (24 acres) in extent, with 14 ponds around its margins for watering stock, and many trees providing shelter. The green was enclosed to produce hay for part of the year, and then opend up for commoners' horses, cattle and, finally, sheep. Grazing was strictly controlled, and on several occasions there were disputes when some farmers attempted to put pigs on the green. Another use of the green was recreation, including football, cricket and an annual fun-fair. This is still one of the finest greens surviving in Oxfordshire.

———◇◇◇———

Map 21 (overleaf) The Thame valley contains a notable group of small parks. Holton is of medieval origin, its centrepiece the moat of the ancient manor-house pulled down in 1808. At Ascott stone gatepiers stand by the roadside at the beginning of a lime avenue which led to the great house of Sir William Dormer, burned down in 1662 before it was ever lived in. Fishponds and garden terraces remain in the derelict park. At Rycote too there are only scanty remains of Sir John Williams' great Tudor brick mansion, which was devastated by fire in 1745, though the medieval chantry chapel with its seventeenth-century interior fittings can still be visited. At Chislehampton the ancient manor-house and church were pulled down by Charles Peers, who replaced them in the 1760s by a new mansion on a different site and a delightful little Georgian chapel on the edge of the park. Perhaps the most interesting of the group is Shotover, where Sir James Tyrrell laid out a formal

*Present-day Oxford High Street in the university
quarter of the city (see also page 80).*

Stanton Harcourt: West Oxfordshire farm labourers' cottages in Sutton Lane, Duck End. Mistletoe Cottage (left) dates from the late seventeenth century, and is built of timber studding and plaster, with stone used only for the wall sills and the gable-end containing the chimney. There were two rooms on the ground floor (one subdivided into pantry and back kitchen), two more within the space beneath the thatched roof, and an attached lean-to hovel for fuel and storage. Pinkhill Cottage (centre) was built as a two-storey house shortly before 1700, timber-framed but with a stone front and chimney wall; later it was subdivided and a second front door inserted. Goldenbridge Cottage (right) is later, probably built around 1845 (see also page 7).

Radcot Bridge in 1987 (see page 72).

Map 21

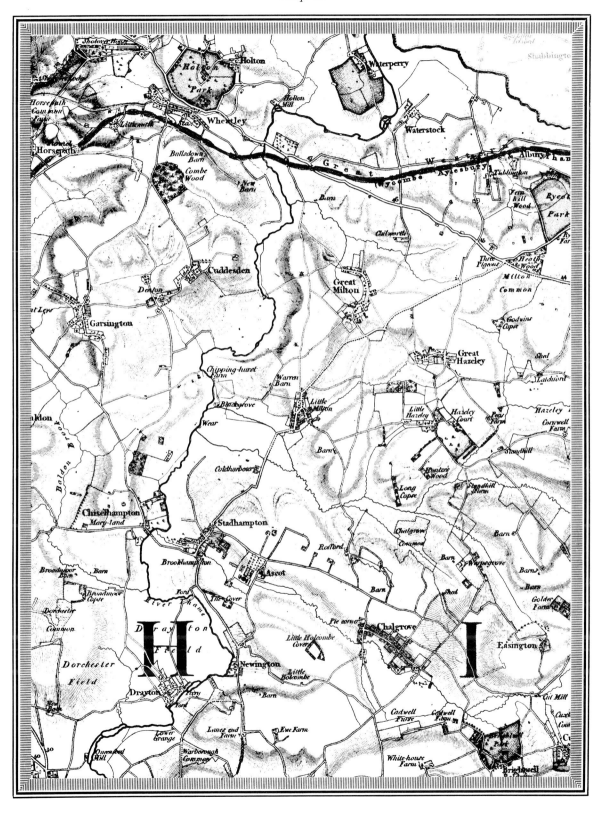

Map 21 cont.

garden in about 1715–18, with a long canal giving a vista to a Gothic folly.

At Chalgrove on 18 June 1643 Prince Rupert defeated a Parliamentarian force led by John Hampden. During the skirmish Hampden was mortally wounded, escaping to Thame where he died six days later. A monument was erected on the battlefield two hundred years later.

———◇◇———

Map 22 The principal market town of the Thame valley is Thame itself, a classic medieval new town laid out over open fields by the Bishop of Lincoln at the beginning of the thirteenth century. Even on a scale of one inch to the mile its regular layout around a great cigar-shaped market place is evident. South of the town the old deer park was given by Bishop Alexander to a community of Cistercian monks who had settled on the edge of Ot Moor in 1138; finding their original site too wet, they moved to Thame two years later, remaining there till the Dissolution. Some of the medieval buildings were incorporated into the Palladian mansion built on the site by Viscount Wenman in the middle of the eighteenth century.

Wheatfield is the site of a deserted village and of the later mansion of the Rudge family,

———

Thame's wide market-place was laid out in the early thirteenth century as part of the Bishop of Lincoln's new town. A thriving market for cattle, sheep, pigs and dairy produce was still continuing here in the nineteenth century (see page 39), and the market was only removed from its ancient site on the main road as recently as 1951.

Map 22

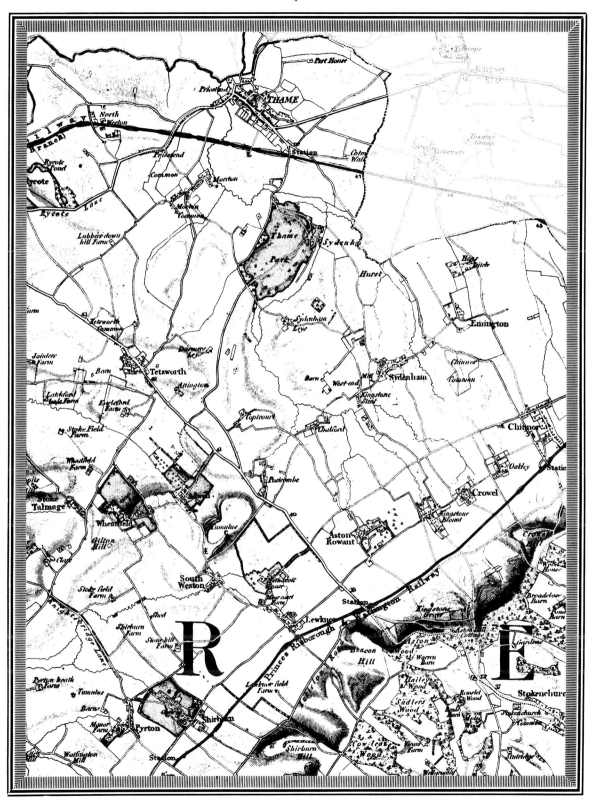

THAME

Post House

Priestend

North Weston

Station

Colmere Walk

Ryecote Pond

Priestend

Ryecote

Common

Moreton

Moreton Common

Thame Park

Sydenham

Hurst

Hog hitch

Lubber down hill Farm

Sydenham Leys

Emmington

Chinnor Common

Tetsworth Common

Farm

Jointers Farm

Barn

Tetsworth

Deepmore

Attington

Barn

West-end

Mill

Sydenham

Chinnor

Latchford Scale Farm

Everlesford Farm

Stoke Field Farm

Topcourt

Kingstone Stait

Chalfont

Oakley

Station

Wheatfield Farm

Postcombe

Crowel

Stoke Talmage

Wheatfield

Tumulus

Aston Rowant

Kingstone Blount

Crest

Wood House

Gilton Hill

Clare

Broadclose Barn

Stoke field Farm

South Weston

Bechholt House

Moorcourt Farm

Station

Kingstone

Aston Hill Cottage

R

Gardens

E

Shirburn Farm

Shut

Lewknor

Wellington Railway

Aston

Wood

Warren Barn

Stonehill Farm

Princes Risborough

Beacon Hill

Hailey Wood

Remlet Wood

Stokenchurch

Pyrton heath farm

Tumulus

Lewknor field Farm

Sadlers Wood

Beast Barn

Stokenchurch Common

Barn

Manor Farm

Pyrton

Shirburn

Shirburn Hill

Cow leaze Wood

Farm

Mill Wood

Clere Hill

Watlington Mill

Station

Wellground

Studridge

Map 22 cont.

itself destroyed by fire in 1814. The stables remain, also the medieval church, now isolated in the park and transformed with stucco, battlements and a Venetian window to conform with early eighteenth-century ideas of landscaping.

Springs rising from the chalk along the scarp foot of the Chilterns have attracted a string of villages from Chinnor to Shirburn and beyond. The moated castle at Shirburn, licensed in 1377, is the first major brick house to be built in Oxfordshire.

Beechwoods on the dip slope of the Chilterns once supported a variety of flourishing woodland industries, particularly the making of chair legs and tent pegs.

Map 23 At Coleshill an ancient moat marks the site of the manor house. Coleshill House was built in 1650 by Sir George Pratt. Great Coxwell, situated on the Corallian beds, is famous for its fourteenth-century tythe barn, built by the monks of Beaulieu and said to be the finest in England. The village of Shrivenham, which sprang up on the road from Swindon to Faringdon, has a twelfth-century church, and Longcott, a settlement on the same road, was enclosed in 1779. Below Shrivenham, the Great Western Railway and the Wilts and Berks Canal enter the county. Compton Beauchamp is a parish situated on Upper Greensand to the west of the Berkshire Ridgeway. Compton House is the sixteenth-century 'old moated grange' described by Hughes in *Tom Brown's Schooldays*. Hardwell Farm has a moated site and Hardwell Camp is a prehistoric monument. The village of Ashbury is situated on the Port Way and within half a mile of the Ridgeway. Wayland Smith's Forge nearby is a neolithic chambered long barrow of sarsen stones, and the subject of a local legend. Ashdown, to the south, also features in legends of King Alfred.

Map 24 (overleaf) Another small village in an area traversed by the Ridgeway, Port Way, the Wilts and Berks Canal and the Great Western Railway, Uffington, in White Horse Vale, has a church dating to *c*1150 and is where Thomas Hughes spent his childhood. Uffington Castle, on the Ridgeway, is an Iron Age fort adjacent to the famous White Horse of the same date, listed as the oldest hill figure in England. A Roman villa was excavated at Woolstone. West and East Challow were ancient settlements associated with the Letcombes. Letcombe Bassett is situated at the head of a deep combe, with three Bronze Age barrows near the village. Letcombe Regis, land held by the Crown in antiquity, had an ancient moat house and a Roman villa. Sparsholt, Childrey and Kingston Lisle are situated on the Port Way, the latter having a blowing stone, again associated with Alfred. To the north Shellingford has a thirteenth-century church and Baulking was first mentioned in AD 948. Near Stanford in the vale stands the nineteenth-century Stanford Place, and at Stanford Farm there are traces of a mansion. Goosey is mentioned in the *Abingdon Chronicles* as being given to the Abbey by King Offa. Letcombe Castle (or Segsbury Camp) is a prehistoric hillfort.

Map 25 (overleaf) Wantage was the birthplace of King Alfred in AD 849. It was made a borough in 1177, and a market place was mentioned in 1284. Cloth was produced there in the fifteenth century and in the eighteenth it had hemp and sacking factories and tanneries. The Wantage Tramway linked with the GWR at Wantage Road Station. In the north, West Hanney is a village surrounding a stone cross, while East Hanney has timbered cottages with overhanging upper storeys. Steventon village is a mile-long paved causeway with seventeenth-century half-timbered houses. East Hendred is one of the

Map 23

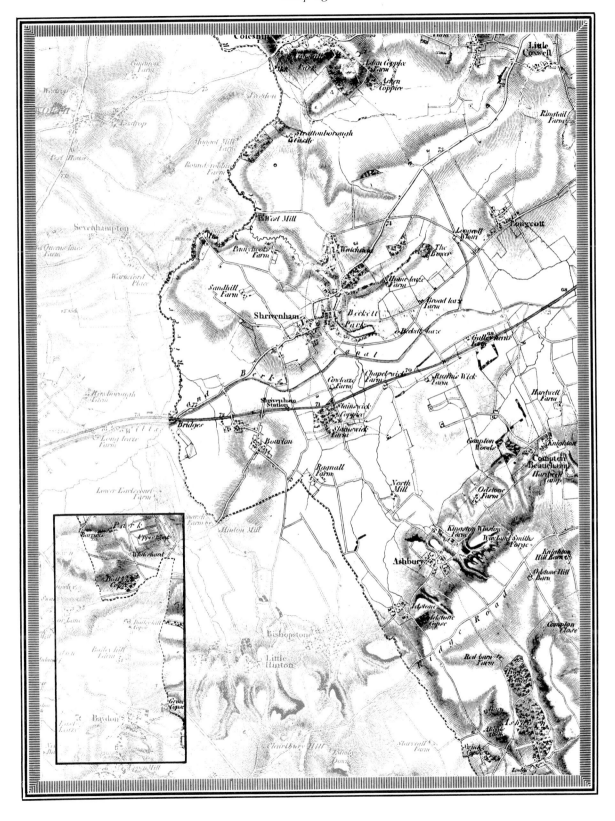

Map 24

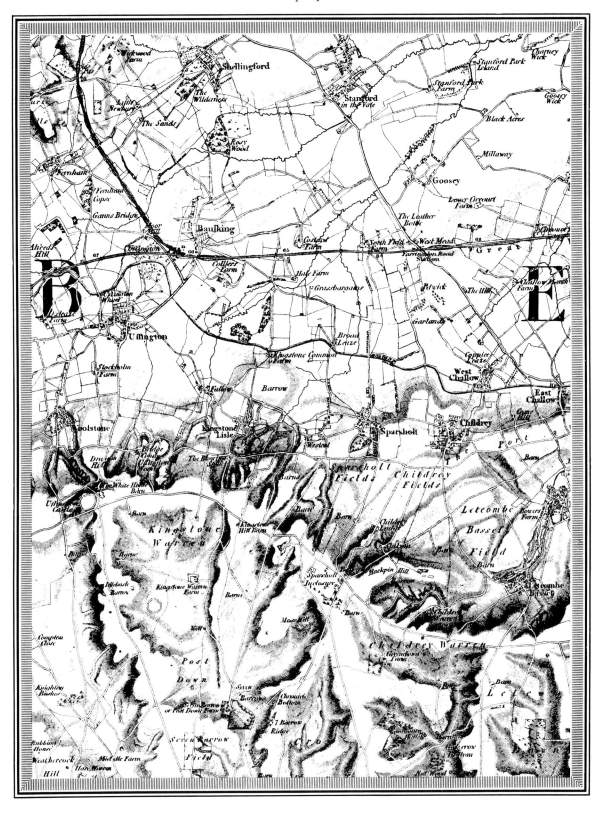

Map 25

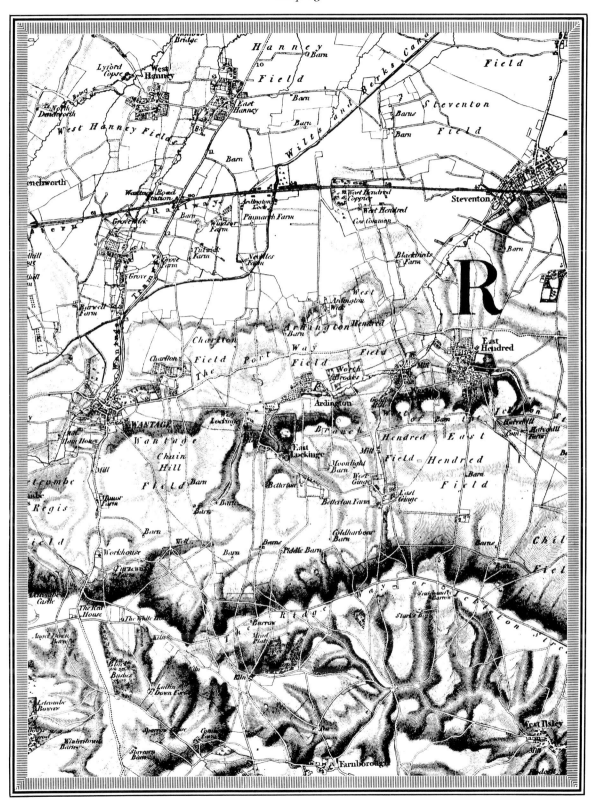

Map 25 cont.

county's most picturesque villages and contains an early fifteenth-century chapel of Jesus of Bethlehem. A weekly market was held there and in the fifteenth century cloth fairs were held on the 'Golden Mile'. Hendred House is the residence of the Eyston family. West Hendred is another attractive settlement. Ardington has a church dating to *c*1200 and Ardington House was built in 1721. West Ilsley is a village in a hollow with Grimsdyke and the Icknield Way to the north. East Lockinge is a modern model village built in 1860 by Lord Wantage. The church is in the park of Lockinge House which was erected in 1750.

The statue of King Alfred in Wantage Market Square at the beginning of this century.

The sleepy downland village of East Hendred (above and top left) looks much the same today as it did in 1917. A few thatched roofs have been replaced by tiling, but otherwise there is little to show that time has passed.

Wantage's most famous inhabitant, King Alfred,
who was born in the town in AD849, surveys the
market square as he did in 1901. During the eighty-
six-year gap he has seen few changes to the buildings,
the arrival of the motor car, and a more permanent
position for his plaque.

Present-day Hurley lock with the changes made to meet the Thames Water Board's requirements (see page 103).

Map 26

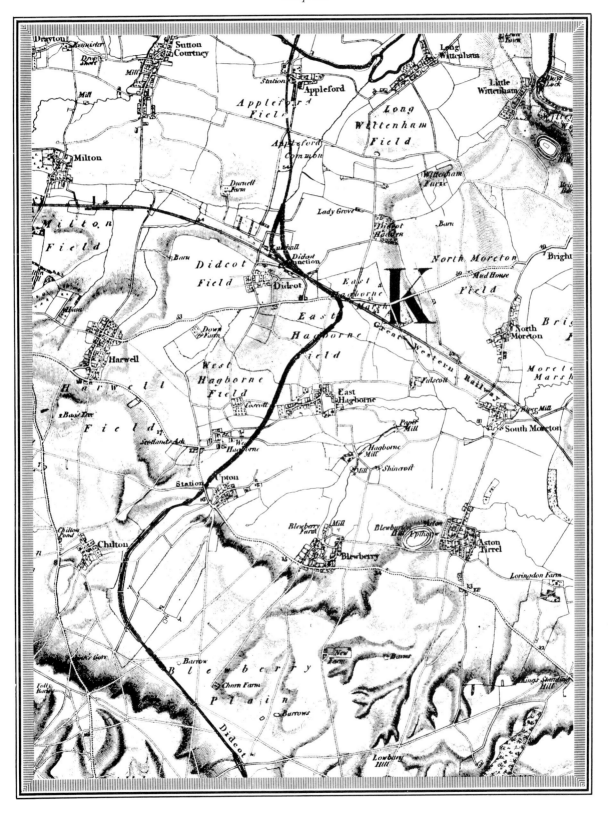

Map 26 (previous page) The Oxford, Didcot and Newbury Railway crosses the area from north to south. Didcot became a junction on the GWR in 1840 and grew from this time. The neighbouring village of Harwell is of ancient origin, but moved into the twentieth century when Britain's first nuclear research station was erected there. In the north, Drayton lies within a triangle of ancient tracks, and Milton House was designed by Inigo Jones in the eighteenth century. Sutton Courtenay has timber-framed buildings of the sixteenth, seventeenth and eighteenth centuries. It was a grange of Abingdon Abbey in the fourteenth century and has a fine Norman Hall dating to the twelfth century. Long Wittenham has a church with a twelfth-century font and piscina and the nearby Wittenham Clumps is comprised of two chalk hills. On Sinodun Hill is a well preserved hillfort above the Thames and Dorchester.

An early GWR locomotive pulls a train from Didcot Junction Station in 1904. The railway brought prosperity to the settlement which was previously little more than a village. As one might expect, the age of the '125' has brought about a degree of modernization to the area.

Upton is a scattered village with wattle-and-daub and half-timbered cottages. There is a moat at Blewbury Farm House and some burial mounds nearby. Blewburton Hillfort was excavated this century. Aston Tirrel, now Aston Tirrold, has a Queen Anne manor house. Brightwell has a moated site and the remnants of a Norman Castle.

Modern map 26 (page 96) The most notable change in this area is the growth of Didcot from a small country village to a medium-sized town. This occurred after the arrival of the railway in 1840 when it was sited on a main route to the west, and was made a junction for both Oxford and Southampton. The Newbury and Southampton branch was later discontinued and replaced by the A34 road which bypasses most settlements on the route. A power station and a trading estate now link Didcot to Milton. Whilst Harwell village remains substantially the same, the Atomic Energy Research Establishment has taken up many many acres of land to the south. To the south of Blewbury modern fieldwork has brought to light much evidence of prehistoric activity in the area of the Ridgeway and many burial mounds have been plotted on this modern map, together with a section of Grim's Ditch which appears regularly in short stretches all over the county. Most other villages remain much as they were 150 years ago.

Map 27 (overleaf) Wallingford dominates this area and the plan of the Saxon town can clearly be seen. Situated on the Thames, the settlement was the principal county borough at the time of the Domesday survey, and receives considerable mention. Wallingford is noted as a Wessex stronghold in the Burghal

Hideage of AD 919. The late ninth-century Saxon town ramparts can still be seen. In the Domesday Book, 491 houses are recorded together with a mint, a market and a guild merchant. The Norman castle occupies a large area in the north-east corner of the town and was used as a royal residence from 1200 to 1385. Wallingford declined before the fourteenth century and never regained its importance. Sotwell, in the north, is a village combined with Brightwell. Moulsford, to the south, was a chapelry of Cholsey until 1847, and is situated on the Roman road that connects Silchester to Dorchester-on-Thames, historically one of the most interesting villages in Oxfordshire. The area was an important religious centre in the neolithic and bronze ages, but the henge and cursus with their associated monuments north and east of the village have been largely destroyed by gravel-

---

Wallingford has many protected buildings and few have changed in this comparison of the Market Place in c1885–95 and the present (see overleaf). The Town Hall, built in 1670, has some minor alterations but still remains a very fine example. A lamp-post, which has been changed into a statue, overlooks the place where markets are still held.

Map 27

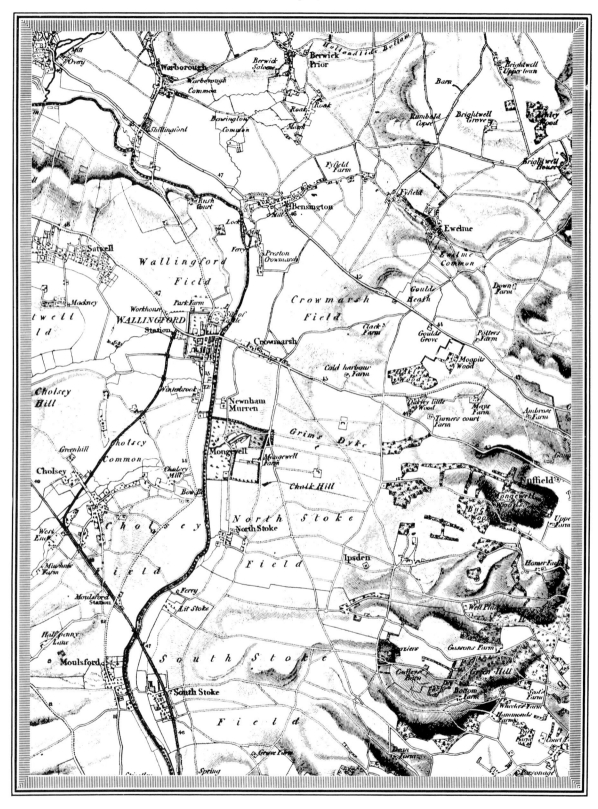

Wallingford Market Place towards the end of the nineteenth century (see page 99).

Map 27 cont.

quarrying. The impressive earthworks of the Dyke Hills, however, a promontory fort dating from the late pre-Roman iron age, can still be seen in the fields to the south-west, while in the village allotments traces of the defences of the Roman town can also be seen. Dorchester was chosen as the site of the first cathedral of the West Saxon kingdom by the missionary Birinus in 635, and it remained an episcopal see until 1080. Some canons remained after the see was transferred to Lincoln, and in 1140 the small community was reorganized as a regular Augustinian abbey. The great abbey church is still the parish church of the village today.

Bensington, now Benson, was the centre of an important royal estate in the Saxon period, which extended in a long strip over the Chilterns as far as Henley.

Much unenclosed land still remained below the Chiltern scarp. The open fields of South Stoke and North Stoke were soon to be enclosed, in 1853 and 1856 respectively, and the commons of Warborough, Benson and Ewelme followed in 1859–63.

Map 28

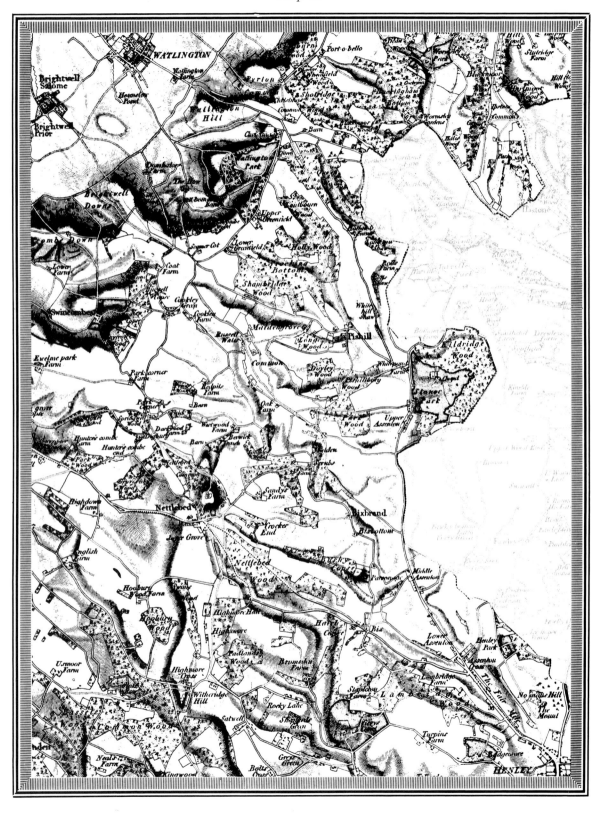

Map 28 The Chiltern landscape is typically one of small hamlets and farms scattered amongst extensive woods and commons. There are few villages, apart from Nettlebed, which had been an important centre of the brick and tile industry since the middle of the fourteenth century. Bricks for the chapel tower at Stonor were made at nearby Crocker End in 1416–17. After the seventeenth century the claypits and kilns around Nettlebed were producing pottery as well as supplying bricks and tiles to a wide area of the Chilterns. By 1880 the whole of Nettlebed Common was pockmarked with claypits. Brick production ceased in 1927, and only a single bottle kiln remains, incongruously marooned on the edge of a modern housing estate.

———◦◦◦———

Map 29 (overleaf) Remenham is a small village on the Thames flood plain at the edge of the Chilterns, and a bridge links it with Henley. At the time of the Domesday Book it belonged to the Crown, and had a chapel under the jurisdiction of Hurley Priory. The priory was founded by Geoffrey de Mandeville in 1086–7, and was endowed with many hides of land. There are considerable remains of the religious building in Hurley village, which has many old cottages together with tythe barns and dovecotes. The crypt of the mansion Ladye Place exists in a private

The river Thames flows past the lock and mill at Hurley c1885–95. Formerly fisheries of the medieval Priory, this stretch of the river has now been modernized. The mill and Mill Cottage have now been demolished (see page 95).

Map 29

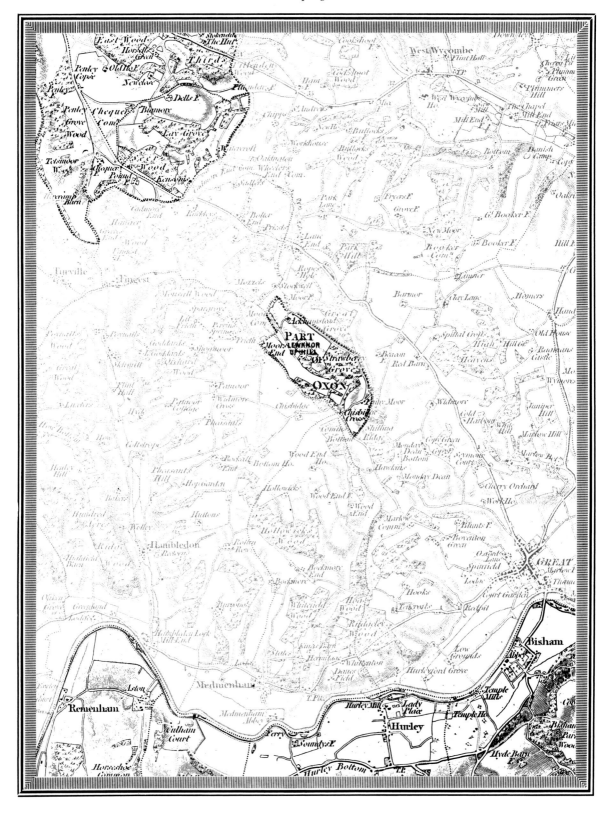

Road signs and cars indicate a modern scene in the village of East Ilsley in the Berkshire Downs (see also page 112).

Present-day Pangbourne Weir (see page 121).

Map 30

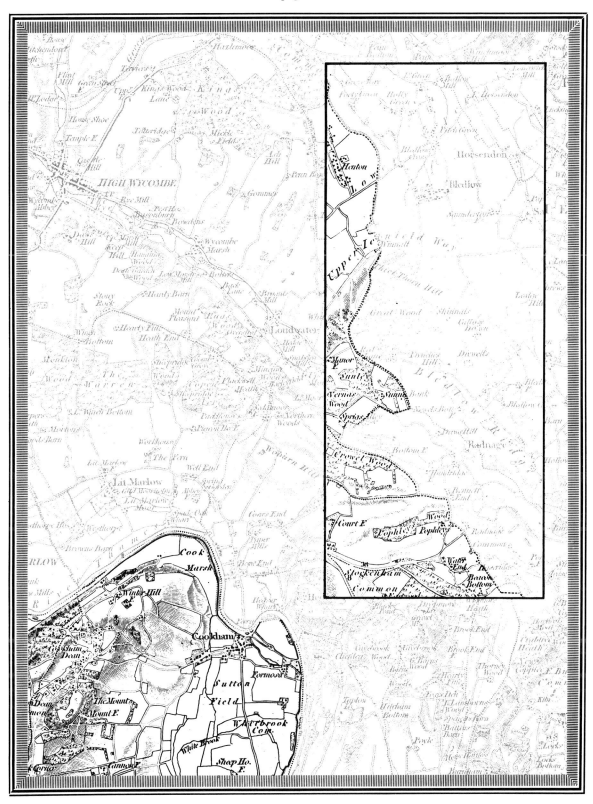

Map 29 cont.

garden. The church is eleventh-century and is connected with the priory. Temple Mills were originally paper mills but have now been demolished. Bisham has a church with a fine Norman tower and some interesting monuments; Bisham Abbey nearby was first used by the Knights Templars, then by the Austin Canons, and after the Dissolution was presented to Anne of Cleeves. Nowadays it is used as a sports centre but retains many historical features.

———⬦○⬦———

Map 30 (page 107) Cookham is an attractive village on the Thames. In Saxon times it was a royal manor and a frontier town between Wessex and Mercia. On Sashes Island near Cookham Lock King Alfred built the fort of Sceaftsege for defence. Its importance in the Anglo-Saxon period is evidenced by the fact that the King called a meeting of the Witan there in AD 997. There was a monastery there by AD 750, and many warrior burials have been excavated in the area. On Cockmarsh there was a group of five barrows of which one contained a Saxon burial. Cockmarsh and Widbrook (Whitebrook) were common lands used by the Abbot of Cirencester in the Middle Ages. The church dates from *c*1150, but could be earlier. Winter Hill is the highest point in the area and affords good views of the Thames and Marlow. Cookham Dean is a later settlement although there is an Iron Age enclosure on Mount Hill.

———⬦○⬦———

Map 31 This area of the Downs has few sizeable settlements except in the valley of the river Lambourn. Running parallel to the valley and to the south is the Roman road, Ermine Street, as it enters from Wiltshire and makes its way to Silchester. Lambourn is the only large town, and the size of its parish suggests that at one time it was the centre of a royal estate. The town was mentioned in

Alfred's will of AD 888 and may have been the site of a royal residence. Lambourn church, the most interesting building in the town, was mentioned in the Domesday Book and in a charter of AD 1090. The town became a borough in 1225. The market cross is all that is left to remind us of the markets which ceased in 1874. The town was modernized in the nineteenth century and today is famous as a centre for horse-training. The Lambourn Seven Barrows is a misnomer for a group of at least twenty Bronze Age burial mounds. To the south Membury hillfort guards the county border, and further down the Lambourn Valley the village of Eastbury is sandwiched between a stone-mullioned manor house and an octagonal dovecote of about 1620. At East Garston thatched cottages are dotted alongside the river.

———⬦○⬦———

Map 32 (overleaf) In the north, Farnborough is situated on an old road running from Hungerford to Abingdon. The village has the stump of a medieval cross and a twelfth-century church. Brightwaltham, or Brightwalton, also has an early church and a moated manor house. The settlement of Chaddleworth surrounds its church on the top of a hill. Nearby is the site of the thirteenth-century Poughley Priory, and a collection of barrows on Woolley Down. Welford and Boxford are villages set in the Lambourn valley. To the east of Boxford 'The Borough' marks the site of an early camp, and at Wyfield Farm nearby a Roman villa was excavated in 1871. Wickham, situated on Ermine Street, is the site of a Roman station. Chieveley, to the east, lies on an ancient route from Oxford to Southampton, and is mentioned in Saxon documents of AD 951.

Map 31

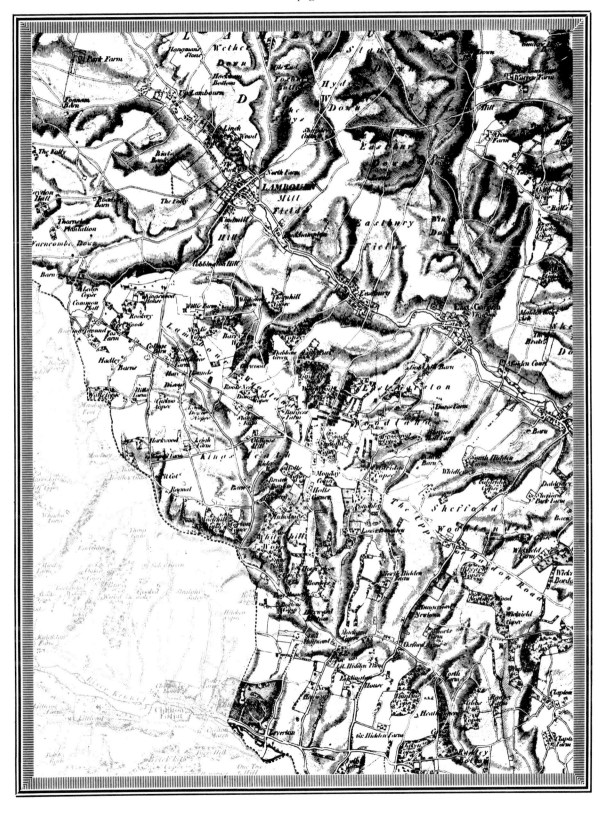

Map 32

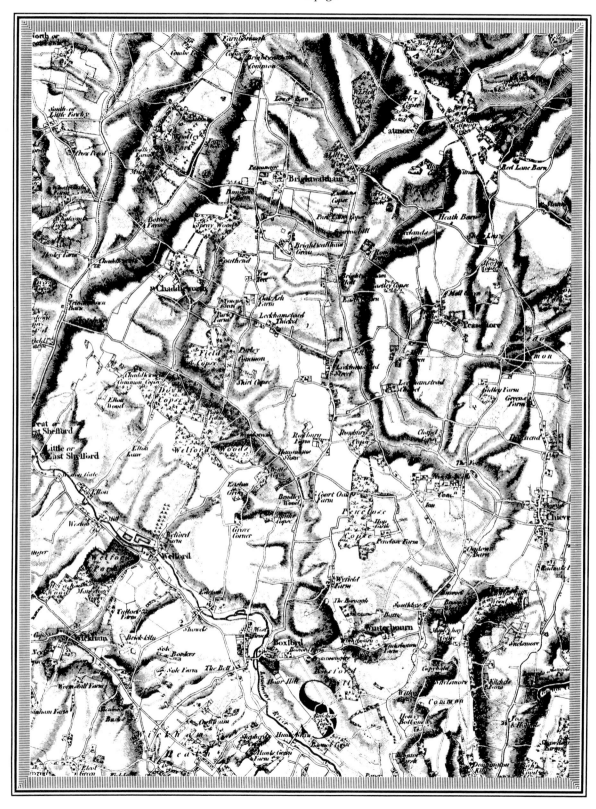

Map 33

Map 33 (page 111) The Newbury to Southampton Railway runs from north to south of this area, meeting the valley of the Pang near Hampstead Norris. East Ilsley, on the Southampton Road, was an important market town in the Middle Ages. Several roads and downland tracks lead to the village, where at times 80,000 sheep per day were auctioned in the market. Today it is more famous for training racehorses. The village is in a hollow, with the church situated on higher ground. Aldworth is a wooded settlement close to the Ridgeway and a section of Grimsdyke. At De La Beche Farm there is an ancient moat. Hampstead Norris, which straddles the Pang, and its neighbour Yattendon, also have connections with the De La Beche family who were manorial lords until 1365. Near Hampstead Norris a Roman villa was discovered at Well House. Another villa was found at Marlston, below Frilsham, a village with a circular churchyard and mill. Bucklebury, a Saxon settlement, is said to be the site of the county residence of the Abbots of Reading, and there are abbey fishponds a quarter of a mile from the church.

Map 34 At Goring the Thames breaks through the chalk escarpment, entering a more constricted section of its course, hemmed in by the Chilterns to the north-east and the Berkshire Downs to the west. Where the wooded hills come down to the riverside meadows there are several fine Tudor brick manor houses set in parks, such as Richard Lybbe's Hardwick Court and Sir Richard Blount's Mapledurham House.

College Wood reminds us of the extensive and distant landholdings of some of the Oxford colleges. In the Middle Ages it had belonged to Eynsham Abbey, and passed to Christ Church after the Dissolution. Woodcote Common to the north was enclosed in 1853, and has since been developed.

Streatley also lies on the Thames and is joined to Goring by a bridge erected in 1838. The Berkshire Ridgeway starts here and joins up with the Icknield Way in Goring Gap. There is much evidence of early settlement and an Anglo-Saxon cemetery was excavated at Southbury Farm. The church is mentioned in the Domesday survey, and there was a mill at Streatley in 1181. Basildon Park, now a National Trust property, is a classical eighteenth-century house. The river Pang joins the Thames at Pangbourne, another early settlement which has yielded Roman and Saxon remains. Hugh Cook, the last Abbot of Reading, is traditionally supposed to have hidden at Bere Court before he was arrested. Further down the Thames Purley Hall is a seventeenth-century building of Portland stone. Tidmarsh is a very wooded parish on the river Pang with a twelfth-century church, and also on the Pang, the village of Bradfield was first mentioned in the seventh century, and has a Roman villa at Maidenhatch Farm. Theale on the old Bath Road has an imposing church of cathedral proportions. Sulham is a village on a wooded hillside and Englefield, whose parish extends from the Pang to the Kennet, was the site of a battle in AD 871. The old Berks and Hants Railway crosses the area south of Theale.

(Previous page) There is little change between this older photograph, taken in 1906, and the present-day village of East Ilsley (see page 105). All roads led to this village in medieval times when it was a centre for sheep marketing.

Map 34

Goring in the late nineteenth century (see page 118).

Willowside, Goring. Goring was still in the late nineteenth century a typical small south Oxfordshire village with timber-framed and brick houses, attractively situated on the Thames beneath wooded downs (see page 116). Opulent villas began to creep out along the riverside in the early years of the present century, and more recently the rail service to London has encouraged the massive expansion of commuter suburbs here.

Cleeve Lock, on the Thames above Goring, 1890 (opposite). In the sixteenth century the navigation passed through a flash-lock in the mill-weir at Cleeve, but this was replaced by a pound-lock in 1787. The lock was rebuilt by the Thames Conservancy in 1874.

One thatched cottage still remains in the village street at Streatley (opposite) as it winds down to the Thames and the Goring Gap. But considering that this is a main road there is little change since the top photograph was taken in c1875–85.

There is a feeling of peace in this scene of Pangbourne Weir and Whitchurch Mill taken c1885–95. In the modern picture (see page 106), taken in the car park of the Swan Inn, the mill has been demolished and the weir modernized. The turbulence of the Thames water appears to emulate the faster pace of modern living.

Map 35

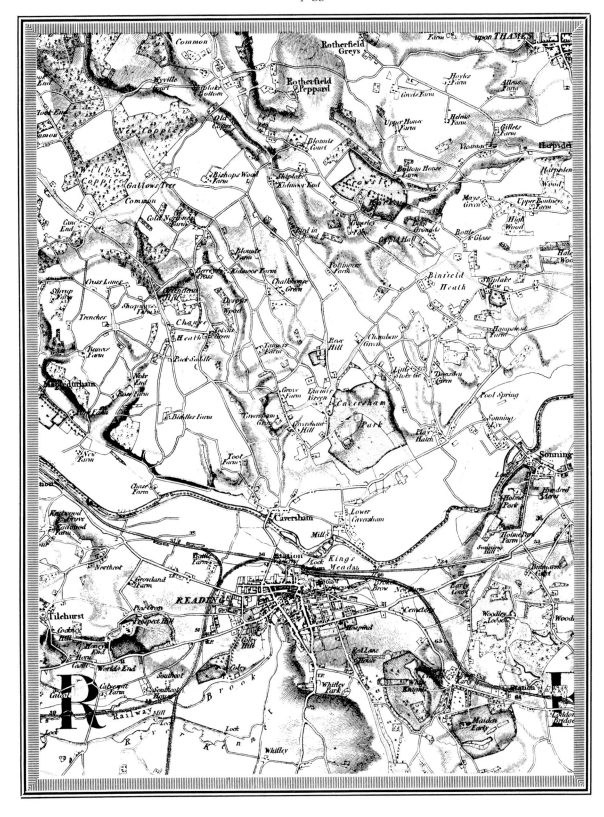